Social Perspectives in the 21st Century

Theories of Aging

New Social Horizons

SOCIAL PERSPECTIVES IN THE 21ST CENTURY

JASON L. POWELL - SERIES AUTHOR –

THE UNIVERSITY OF CHESTER, U.K.

Theories of Aging: New Social Horizons
Jason L. Powell and Sheying Chen
2020. 978-1-53617-079-5

Life Course and Society
Jason L. Powell
2018. ISBN: 978-1-53613-848-1

The Power of Global Aging
Jason L. Powell
2018. ISBN: 978-1-53613-846-7

Feminist Social Theory
Jason L. Powell
2014. ISBN: 978-1-62948-535-5

Power and Aging: A Macro and Micro Analysis
Jason L. Powell
2014. ISBN: 978-1-62948-534-8

Theorizing Community Care: From Disciplinary Power to Governmentality to Personal Care
Jason L. Powell
2014. ISBN: 978-1-62948-532-4

The "Management of Aging" and the Dark Side of Modernity
Jason L. Powell
2014. ISBN: 978-1-62948-533-1

Aging, Culture and Society: A Sociological Approach
Jason L. Powell
2013. ISBN: 978-1-62808-960-8

Aging, Risk and Globalization
Jason L. Powell
2013. ISBN: 978-1-62808-902-8

**Contemporary Issues in
Modern Society**
Jason L. Powell
2013. ISBN: 978-1-62808-212-8

**Education, Employment
and Pensions:
A Critical Narrative**
Jason L. Powell
2013. ISBN: 978-1-62808-383-5

**From Historical Social Theory
to Foucault**
Jason L. Powell
2013. ISBN: 978-1-62618-345-2

**Global Aging, China
and Urbanization**
Jason L. Powell
2013. ISBN: 978-1-62808-452-8

**Helping Professions and Aging:
Theory, Policy
and Practice**
Jason L. Powell
2013. ISBN: 978-1-62808-381-1

**Issues in Crime, Criminal Justice
and Aging**
Jason L. Powell
2013. ISBN: 978-1-62808-890-8

Issues in Sociology
Jason L. Powell
2013. ISBN: 978-1-62808-211-1

Key Thinkers in Social Science
Jason L. Powell
2013. ISBN: 978-1-62808-453-5

**Neo-Liberalism and the Power of
Globalization**
Jason L. Powell
2013. ISBN: 978-1-62948-469-3

Rethinking Social Welfare
Jason L. Powell
2013. ISBN: 978-1-62808-330-9

**Social Philosophy,
Age and Aging**
Jason L. Powell
2013. ISBN: 978-1-62808-382-8

**Social Work, Performativity and
Personalization**
Jason L. Powell
2013. ISBN: 978-1-62808-903-5

Symbolic Interactionism
Jason L. Powell
2013. ISBN: 978-1-62808-213-5

The Aging Body
Jason L. Powell
2013. ISBN: 978-1-62808-380-4

**The Social Analysis of Emotion
and Trust**
Jason L. Powell
2013. ISBN: 978-1-62948-120-3

**Understanding Foucault:
For Beginners**
Jason L. Powell
2013. ISBN: 978-1-62417-195-6

**Understanding Power and
Emotion: An Introduction**
Jason L. Powell
2013. ISBN: 978-1-62417-200-7

**Understanding Risk and Trust:
A Short Conceptual Examination**
Jason L. Powell
2013. ISBN: 978-1-62417-202-1

Baudrillard and Postmodernism
Jason L. Powell
2012. ISBN: 978-1-62257-541-1

Feminism
Jason L. Powell
2012. ISBN: 978-1-62257-540-4

Foucault: Issues and Legacy
Jason L. Powell
2012. ISBN: 978-1-62257-539-8

Habermas
Jason L. Powell
2012. ISBN: 978-1-62257-542-8

SOCIAL PERSPECTIVES IN THE 21ST CENTURY

THEORIES OF AGING

NEW SOCIAL HORIZONS

JASON L. POWELL
AND
SHEYING CHEN

Copyright © 2020 by Nova Science Publishers, Inc.

All rights reserved. No part of this book may be reproduced, stored in a retrieval system or transmitted in any form or by any means: electronic, electrostatic, magnetic, tape, mechanical photocopying, recording or otherwise without the written permission of the Publisher.

We have partnered with Copyright Clearance Center to make it easy for you to obtain permissions to reuse content from this publication. Simply navigate to this publication's page on Nova's website and locate the "Get Permission" button below the title description. This button is linked directly to the title's permission page on copyright.com. Alternatively, you can visit copyright.com and search by title, ISBN, or ISSN.

For further questions about using the service on copyright.com, please contact:
Copyright Clearance Center
Phone: +1-(978) 750-8400   Fax: +1-(978) 750-4470   E-mail: info@copyright.com.

NOTICE TO THE READER

The Publisher has taken reasonable care in the preparation of this book, but makes no expressed or implied warranty of any kind and assumes no responsibility for any errors or omissions. No liability is assumed for incidental or consequential damages in connection with or arising out of information contained in this book. The Publisher shall not be liable for any special, consequential, or exemplary damages resulting, in whole or in part, from the readers' use of, or reliance upon, this material. Any parts of this book based on government reports are so indicated and copyright is claimed for those parts to the extent applicable to compilations of such works.

Independent verification should be sought for any data, advice or recommendations contained in this book. In addition, no responsibility is assumed by the Publisher for any injury and/or damage to persons or property arising from any methods, products, instructions, ideas or otherwise contained in this publication.

This publication is designed to provide accurate and authoritative information with regard to the subject matter covered herein. It is sold with the clear understanding that the Publisher is not engaged in rendering legal or any other professional services. If legal or any other expert assistance is required, the services of a competent person should be sought. FROM A DECLARATION OF PARTICIPANTS JOINTLY ADOPTED BY A COMMITTEE OF THE AMERICAN BAR ASSOCIATION AND A COMMITTEE OF PUBLISHERS.

Additional color graphics may be available in the e-book version of this book.

Library of Congress Cataloging-in-Publication Data

ISBN: 978-1-53617-079-5

Published by Nova Science Publishers, Inc. † New York

CONTENTS

Preface		ix
Chapter 1	Introduction: The Social Construction of Aging and Old Age	1
Chapter 2	Theorizing Embodiment, Postmodernism and Aging	23
Chapter 3	Towards a Narrative Gerontology	49
Chapter 4	Conclusion: Towards Global Theories of Aging	65
References		79
Authors' Contact Information		109
Index		111
Related Nova Publications		115

PREFACE

This innovative book is a theoretical, reflexive and critical overview of the key issues connected to aging in contemporary society. The book explores how aging has been theorized which has increasing implications for socio-economic issues for individuals and populations. The book also explores the interaction between method-theory dualism through the concept of narrative which is quickly on its way to becoming the most context sensitive analytical frameworks to examine instances of aging identity. Related to this, the book then explores some of the major impacts on embodiment and how it impinges on aging identity. Contentiously, the biggest social horizon for gerontologists to grapple with are global interpretations of aging which along with climate change is one of the greatest sustainable challenges for every nation states across the globe requiring not just critical questions but research informed solutions. We hope the book is both inspiring and enriching for researchers, teachers, students, practitioners and policy makers both nationally and internationally.

Chapter 1

INTRODUCTION: THE SOCIAL CONSTRUCTION OF AGING AND OLD AGE

This book is about deconstructing assumptions of aging and old age through the theoretical prisms of social gerontology which is also about illuminating new social horizons based on theoretical development, theory-method dualism, embodiment and identity and the global implications of aging. There has long been a propensity in matters of aging and old age to engage in the reductionism of aging to its biological and psychological dimensions. Indeed, in Western culture, aging came to be understood in terms of biological science to be only material, and the scientific approach to medicine became overwhelmingly objective, reductionistic, and rational. These scientific dimensions primarily are a set of normative "stages" of body and mind processes that position the experiences and representations of aging and old age in Western culture (Gilleard and Higgs 2000). For the biomedical model, growing old would primarily be a process of inevitable physical and mental "decline" and of preparation for the ultimate ending: death itself. The paradox, of course, is that the biomedical homogenizing of the experience of old age which the reliance on the biological and psychological dimensions of aging entails, is in fact one of the key elements of the (public) dominant "commonsense" discourses on aging and old age. A deeper understanding of aging requires, however, that we move beyond commonsense approaches and broaden our view to understand how processes, from the biomedical level of the individual cell to overall society, influence us, and in turn are influenced by us as individuals progressing through the life course.

The social construction of aging is an important process in debunking discourses of "truth" and can be used as an alternative to narrow medical narratives (Powell 2002); it includes how "norms" or pervasive attitudes materialize—from basic biomedical functions to sophisticated and complex social/cultural structures including educational, political, and religious institutions, the arts, customs, morality, ethics, and law.

Social constructs are enormously powerful in determining individual and collective identity. Those in power present ontologically arbitrary social constructs as "the way life actually is," that is, as reality. For example, biomedical sciences have been important in this process in shaping reality regarding the aging process. The social constructions of aging assert that aging has no existence independent of social interaction and power relationships in society; they are not grounded in "nature" as is biomedical gerontology under the auspices of biological-psychological gerontological knowledge (the meaning of which is itself socially determined). Indeed, the constructedness of aging is made invisible by the normal workings of social life, so that it appears natural rather than artificial. Social constructionism is therefore about helping individuals to stand outside their own prejudices and see the notion of the "other" in order to explain and understand what may be happening in the social world, given that reality is increasingly seen as fragile, shifting, and coexisting with different "realities." Further, embracing the social construction of aging can help individuals blame themselves less for their "problems" and strive to change limiting biomedical discourses of human behavior.

The promise of a sociology of aging then could transcend narrow biomedical explanations; it might take a cue from C. Wright Mills's tour de force *The Sociological Imagination* (1959). Mills suggested that the promise and responsibility of the discipline of sociology lie in giving individuals the conceptual tools to make distinctions between "personal troubles" and "public issues." Social theorists can make this distinction if they have a

Introduction

3

social context and a sense of history from which to understand personal experiences.

The ability to shift perspectives, to analyze an experience or an issue from many levels of analysis and to see the intersection of these levels and mutual influence, is the heart of the sociological imagination. If we develop a new understanding of our own attitudes about aging because we learn about how societies construct meanings of age, then we will have experienced the "sociological imagination." As Mills (1959, 5) points out: "No social study that does not come back to the problem of biography, of history and of their intersections within a society has completed its intellectual journey."

With these "tools for thinking," Mills focuses our attention on the broad social structures that shape our personal stories. Equipped with this understanding, we can go on to understand how "by the fact of our living, we contribute, however minutely, to the shaping of our society and the course of history, even as we are made by society and its historical push" (Mills 1959, 4). In order to understand aging we need to be aware of how our personal knowledge is shaped by ourselves and by society as a whole.

Drawing from this definition and process of the "sociological imagination" and the interplay between social context and individuals; the sociology of aging can be defined as the systematic study of the taken-for-granted assumptions that are socially constructed by society and filter through to shape personal attitudes about aging in everyday life. The sociology of aging is also the study of the relationships between institutions and individuals in society. The sociology of aging provides an analytical framework for understanding the interplay between human lives and changing social structures. Sociologists are interested, therefore, in how society works, the arrangements of its structure and institutions, and the mechanisms of its processes of change.

Hence, the sociology of aging is important in examining the interdependence between aging over the life-course as a social process and societies and groups as classified by age. The field of social gerontology contributes to it through reformulation of traditional emphases on process and change and on the multidimensionality of sociological concerns as they touch on related aspects of other social science disciplines (Chen and Powell 2011).

The field of social gerontology is concerned with both basic sociological research on age and its implications for social theory as well as policy and professional practice. Nevertheless—and it is almost an embarrassing statement to make—as a field of study, mainstream sociology has not been interested in the sociology of aging (Powell 2002). As Powell (2011) points out, in male-dominated sociology the study of aging has been seen as one of the lowest-status areas of all. Despite the poverty of theory in social gerontology in recent years (Bengston, Burgess, and Parrot 1997), this chapter interrogates and problematizes the ways social theories have arisen in relation to interpretations of aging, with particular focus to American and British social gerontology.

This chapter focuses on highlighting the major theoretical schools in social gerontology by addressing functionalist gerontology, political economy of old age, and feminist gerontology. It is arguable that these three theoretical models of aging are dominant in modernist constructions of knowledge of aging, but they remain important reference points about the nature of aging and its structural, interpersonal, and esoteric constructions. The chapter then introduces two essential identity variables that have been historically omitted as to fully understanding the complexity of aging in modernity: race and sexuality.

THE GAZE OF FUNCTIONALIST GERONTOLOGY

In the postwar years, social gerontology emerged as a multidisciplinary field of study that attempted to respond to the social, health, and economic policy implications and projections of populational change in Western society (Phillipson 1998). The disciplinary subject matter of social gerontology encompassed a wide range of social science approaches (economic, political science, and human geography, as well as sociology) that was shaped by significant external forces: first, by state intervention to achieve specific outcomes in health and social policy for older people;

Introduction 5

secondly, by a sociopolitical and economic setting that viewed an aging population as creating a "social problem" for Western society in general (Phillipson 1998).

However, it was not until the 1950s that social analysis of aging began to emerge in its own right. In the United States, it is significant that this growth was underpinned by the involvement and interest of notable functionalist sociologists who helped lay the foundations for the rapid growth of the discipline between the 1950s and 1975.

In postwar Great Britain, by contrast, social research on old age was largely subsumed within the wider concerns of the expanding welfare state, and it has only recently emerged as a field of academic study in its own right. Considerable shifts in socioeconomic policy and demographic changes have set the stage for what is an increasingly important debate on the interpretation of aging. Until the 1990s, not only was age subsumed under race, class, and gender, but the dominant explanatory framework concerning aging came, as we discussed earlier, from outside of sociology: the so-called medical model. So it is of central importance that aging came to be looked at in social terms.

The important point to note is that theories often mirror the norms and values of their creators and their social times, reflecting culturally dominant views of what should be the appropriate way to analyze social phenomena (Kalish 1979; Turner 1989). The two functionalist theories that dominated U.S. gerontology in the 1950s and 1960s, the disengagement and activity theories, follow this normative pattern. Both disengagement and activity theories not only postulate how individual behavior changes with aging, but also imply how it should change.

Disengagement Theory

Functionalist sociology dominated the sociological landscape in the United States from the 1930s until the 1960s (Blaikie 1999). In the 1940s, functionalist gerontologists were already obsessed with the consequences of role loss among older people. Old age, characterized as a "roleless role"

(Cumming and Henry 1961) was seen as a period of life in which feelings of dissatisfaction and low morale prevailed. However, as Dowd points out, the antidote to these "miseries" became part of standard gerontological wisdom by the early 1950s: remain active and make creative uses of leisure time. To this way of thinking, meaning is imposed from the outside and resides primarily in societal tasks and duties such as work and childrearing. Except for some concern for the socially isolating aspects of physical frailty, the body was not a major concern of these scholars.

This view of aging appeared in the United States in the dominant - structural-functionalist school via the work of "disengagement theorists" (Phillipson 1998). Such major protagonists of disengagement theory were Cumming and Henry (1961), who looked at how older people should disengage from work roles and prepare for the ultimate disengagement: death (Powell 2000, 2001a). They also proposed that gradual withdrawal of older people from work roles and social relationships is both an "inevitable" and "natural" process: "withdrawal may be accompanied from the outset by an increased preoccupation with himself: certain institutions may make it easy for him" (Cumming and Henry 1961, 14).

Cumming and Henry (1961) maintained that the process of disengagement (an inevitable, rewarding, and universal process of mutual withdrawal of the individual and society from each other with advancing age) was normal and to be expected. This theory argued that it was beneficial for both the aging individual and society that such disengagement take place in order to minimize the social disruption caused by an aging person's eventual death (Neugarten, 1996). Cumming and Henry's disengagement theory of aging proclaims that the aged individuals must be deposed from their various roles for the proper functioning of the society. According to the proponents of this theory, disengagement is a gradual and an inevitable process. Moreover, disengagement theory confines the area of operation of the aged by restricting their scope for employment and commitments. In essence, though controversial, the theory is normative in claiming that disengagement of older people is functional—it offers psychological well-being to older individuals (Cumming and Henry 1961).

Introduction 7

Retirement is an example of the disengagement process, enabling older persons to be freed of the roles of an occupation and to pursue other roles not necessarily aligned with generating income. Through disengagement, Cumming and Henry (1961) argued, society anticipated the loss of aging people through death and brought "new blood" into full participation within the social world.

Bronley (1966, quoted in Bond and Coleman 1993, 43) further asserts that "in old age, the individual is normally disengaged from the main streams of economic and community activity."

Not surprisingly for Bromley (1966, quoted in Bond and Coleman 1993, 44): "The (disengagement) process is graded to suit the declining biological and psychological capacities of the individual and the needs of society."

In order to legitimize its macrogeneralizations, disengagement theory boasted of the objective and value-free rigor of its research, citing its survey and questionnaire methods of gerontological inquiry. In a sense, arguing for disengagement from work roles under the guise of objectivity, based on scientific method, gives governments a very powerful argument for legitimizing the definitions of who can work and who cannot, based on age (Powell 1999).

Activity Theory

The second functionalist theory, activity theory, is a counterpoint to disengagement theory, since it claims that a successful old age can be achieved only by maintaining roles and relationships (Powell 2001). Activity theory actually predates disengagement theory. In the 1950s Havighurst and Albrecht (1953, cited in Katz 1996) insisted aging can be a lively and creative experience. For activity theorists, disengagement is not a natural process, as advocated by Cumming and Henry. For activity theorists, disengagement theory is inherently ageist and does not promote, in any shape or form, "positive aging" (Estes, Biggs, and Phillipson 2003).

The activity theory of aging, developed by Havighurst, B. Neugarten and Tobin (Powell 2000), has developed a different approach for the elderly in modern society. According to Powell (2001c), this theory is regarded as an anti-aging perspective and maintains that, if the roles and activities associated with old age are lost, it is important to develop a new set of roles and activities in order to replace them. Thus, replacement of roles and activities is compulsory for the aged because it enhances their life satisfaction. In fact, the activity theory can best be attributed to the perspective of emancipation.

The point here is that old age was understood to be a uniform process and a uniformly problematic and depressing state. Older persons' only hope for contentment lay in increasing their level of social activity.

Nevertheless, activity theory neglects issues of power, inequality, and conflict between age groups. An apparent "value consensus" may reflect the interests of powerful and dominant groups within society who find it advantageous to have age/power relations organized in such a way. While Phillipson (1998) sees such functionalist schools as important in shaping social theory responses to them, such functionalist theories impose a sense of causality on aging by implying that one will either "disengage" or will be "active" in old age. Such theories of aging are very macro-oriented and fail to resolve tensions within age-group relations that impinge upon the interconnection of race, class, and gender with age (Powell 1999).

POLITICAL ECONOMY OF OLD AGE AND THE POLITICS OF DISTRIBUTION

"Political economy of old age" was coined (cf. Estes 1979) as a critical response to theoretical dominance of functionalism and the epistemic normative explanatory frameworks: either disengage or be active. Political economy of old age emerged as a critical orthodoxy that focused on how the state and its resources and institutions positioned the experiences and life-chances of older people in capitalist Western society (Phillipson 1998).

Arguably, this critical branch of political economic gerontology grew as a direct response to the hegemonic dominance not only of structural

Introduction 9

functionalism, in the form of disengagement/activity theories, but also of the biomedical paradigm and the world economic crises of the 1970s. As Phillipson (1998) points out, in the United Kingdom huge blocks of social expenditure were allocated to older people. Consequently, not only were older people viewed in medical terms but in resource terms by governments. This brought a new perception to attitudes to age and aging. In the United Kingdom, the William Beveridge post–World War II vision of universal access to welfare services was under sustained attack. As Phillipson (1998, 17) teases out: "Older people came to be viewed as a burden on western economies, with demographic change seen as creating intolerable pressures on public expenditure."

A major concern of "political economy of old age" thinking was to challenge both the epistemological dominance of functionalist thought and the biomedical models of age and aging. The political economy approach wanted to have "an understanding of the character and significance of variations in the treatment of the aged, and to relate these to polity, economy and society in advanced capitalist society" (Estes 1986, 7).

The major focus is an interpretation of the relationship between aging and the economic structure. In the United States, political economy of old age was pioneered in the work of Caroll L. Estes (1979) and Minkler and Estes (1998), for example. Similarly, in the United Kingdom, the work of Alan Walker (1981, 1985), Peter Townsend (1981), and Chris Phillipson (1982, 1998) added a critical sociological dimension to understanding age and aging in advanced capitalist societies. For Estes (1979) the class structure is targeted as the key determinant of the position of older people in capitalist society. For Minkler and Estes (1998), political economy challenges the ideology of older people as belonging to a homogenous group unaffected by dominant structures in society.

Estes and Associates (2001) claim political economy focuses upon an analysis of the state in contemporary societal formations. Here, we can see how Marxism is interconnected to this theory. Estes and Associates (2001) look to how the state decides and dictates who is allocated resources and who is not. This impinges upon retirement and subsequent pension schemes.

Phillipson (1982, 1998) supplements this by suggesting that the retirement experience, linked to the timing of reduction of wages and enforced withdrawal from work, has put many older people in the U.K. in a financially insecure position. Hence, the state can make and break the fortunes of its populace. Consequently, current governmental discourses about cutting public expenditure on pensions and increasingly calling for private provision of support for the aged legitimizes the ideological mystification stereotypes of "burden" groups and populations. This is a case of the state using its power to transfer responsibility of pension provision from the state and onto individuals. Indeed, blaming people for nonprovision of their own savings obscures and mystifies the fact that real economic problems derive from the capitalist mode of production and political decisions.

We can see that political economy is a "grand" theory drawing from Marxian historiography; it locates the determining explanatory factors in the structure of society and focuses upon welfare and its contribution to the institutional decommodification of retired older people. Ageist attitudes toward older people and their often impoverished position are best explained by their loss of social worth resulting from the loss of their productive roles in a society that puts a premium on production (Estes, Swan, and Gerard 1982).

Townsend (1981) further observes that society creates the social problems of old age through "structured dependency" embedded in institutional ageism: poverty due to lack of material resources, retirement policies, negative consequences of residential care, and passive forms of community care services. Townsend focuses on a "structural" perspective of "rules and resources" governing older people in advanced capitalism and wider social system.

Similarly, Alan Walker (1981) has argued passionately for a political economy of old age in order to understand the marginal position of older people. In particular, Walker (1981, 77) paid attention to the "social creation of dependency" and how social structure and relations espoused by the mode of production helps intensify structural class marginalization. In a similar vein, Phillipson (1982, 1988) considers how capitalism helps socially

Introduction 11

construct the social marginality of older people in key areas such as welfare delivery. The important argument to be made is that inequalities in the distribution of resources should be understood in relation to the distribution of power within society and social class, rather than in terms of individual variation.

Political economy still retains an influence in gerontological theorizing but has reframed and renamed itself as "critical gerontology" (Phillipson 1998). Critical gerontology is a perspective whereby genuine knowledge is based on the involvement of the "objects" of study in its definition and results in a positive vision of how things might be better, rather than an understanding of how things actually are (Phillipson 1998). As suggested, "critical gerontology" grew out of political economy of old age; political economy was criticized for being overly concerned with "structured dependency" (Walker 1981) brought on by social and economic disadvantage and its implicit determinism that can see older people as passive, even insentient beings. Critical gerontology is still concerned with structural inequalities, but it is interested in moral concepts; it has a commitment not only to understanding marginality but also to challenging it. A reflexive critical gerontology also pays more attention to human agency and social class and the way in which individuals both influence the world around them and modify their behavior in response to information from the world in neoliberal contemporary modernity.

For example, from the 1980s on, the neoliberal dominance in social policy has been very successful because it has identified existential concepts such as self-responsibility, self-governance, and self-care that are said to facilitate social action (Leonard 1997). The regulation of personal conduct has shifted from being presented as "structured dependency" by the state (Walker 1981) to the responsibility of "older people" as "consumers" (Phillipson 1998). Since the 1980s, the nature of society is contested hotly by neoliberalism, with its central belief in the virtue of small government, especially in the economic sphere of life. For Estes, Biggs, and Phillipson (2004) the perception for neoliberals is that governments should intervene in markets only when the intervention is less damaging than the consequences of market failure. Where intervention is needed, it should be the minimum possible. If feasible, neoliberal governments should retain market exchanges in social welfarism. Quasi-market solutions should be favored over command solutions. The direct assumption of responsibility for the production of goods and services by government is almost never accepted except for the few special exemptions such as: national defense and maintaining law and order.

Under neoliberalism, the state reinvents itself and its welfare subjects based upon minimal intervention and regulation via a rolling program of privatization, deregulation, and contraction of welfare services (Estes and Associates 2001). Within the mixed economy of welfare there has been the social construction of a market oriented, consumer based approach to the delivery of care. As Peter Leonard (1997) claims, the neoliberal state is being reorganized to include a retention of a strong center to formulate policy but with the dissemination of responsibility for policy implementation to managerial regimes. As Gordon (1991, 36) points out: "The fulfillment of the liberal idea is a recasting of the interface between the state and society to one of market order. It becomes the ambition of neo-liberalism to implicate individuals as players into the market game administered by managerial actors."

Such a development is framed in the language of the market, as opposed to social scientific discourse, although negative stereotyping can be brought in from time to time to reinforce an individualized or stigmatized notion of structured dependency. New neoliberal policy priorities on consumerism require new technologies if they are to influence both the control of resources and the "hearts and minds" of their objects. But for Chris Phillipson (1998), consumerist ideas in modern society ignore the experiences of older people, especially with regard to poverty and social deprivation. This is an enduring theme. After engaging in a series of qualitative and quantitative observations on older people in preindustrial and industrial societies, Powell (2001c) portrays a sense of the abandonment of the role of older people in neoliberal society. Modernity has failed to give due recognition to older people; the older you become, the more you experience a sense of relative deprivation. Fundamentally, the risk of hardship for the aging in modernity is exacerbated through neoliberal ideas

Introduction

13

of cutting state finance and enforcing people to use their own funds in the management of their own welfare. Indeed, Powell (2000) claims that neoliberalism at surface level consistently equates self-responsibility with freedom and sees people as active agents in consumer market. However, social class as a structural shaper and mover of society may leave many poorer older people in a vulnerable, "choiceless" position in social welfare; despite the neoliberal menu of rights, self-responsibility, and "freedoms" equated with becoming a "responsible consumer." Both the Cameron and to a lesser extent Obamagovernments have spoken about the need for private pensions and has constantly reinforced this point by saying that effects of an "aging population" will mean that public finances could not fund a full pension, and older people and families must be more "responsible" with saving for pensions (Powell and Wahidin 2004). However, we have seen the effect of private pension schemes, especially in the United Kingdom; a report by the Office of Fair Trading (1997) found that up to £4 billion had been lost by pensioners in private pension schemes, according to *The Times* "the greatest financial scandal of the century." Then came the discovery after the death of Robert Maxwell that he had embezzled £400 million from his companies' pension schemes (Powell and Wahidin 2004).

"Critical gerontology" has had an enormous impact on theorizing about aging in recent years (Phillipson 1998). This approach to capitalist societies' treatment of older people has overemphasized class relations (Turner 1989) and neglected the differences between capitalist societies (Boneham and Blakemore 1994). More recently, attention has been paid to ways in which capitalist societies structure age relations in terms of gender (Arber and Ginn 1991, 1995) and race and ethnicity (Boneham and Blakemore 1994). Indeed, this theoretical approach reifies "older age" by discounting the potential for improvements in the social situation of older people (Featherstone and Hepworth 1993). Further, Wahidin and Powell (2003) ask why macrotheory overlooks both ontological and epistemological issues associated with the "aging body." This is an important question that will be addressed in chapter 5.

FEMINIST INTERPRETATIONS OF AGING AND GENDER

In recent years, there has been an acceleration of feminist insights into understanding age and gender as entwined identity variables of analysis (Arber and Ginn 1991, 1995). There are two important issues: first, power imbalances shape theoretical construction; second, a group's place within the social structure influences the theoretical attention that they are afforded. Therefore, because older women tend to have lower class status, especially in terms of economics, than men of all ages and younger women, they are given less theoretical attention (Arber and Ginn 1995). Although in recent years there has been a small but growing body of evidence in mainstream sociological theory the interconnection of age and gender has been undertheorized and overlooked. In recent years, there has been an acceleration of feminist insights into understanding age and gender as identity variables of analysis (Arber and Ginn 1991, 1995). Finch (1986) agrees that the epistemological failure to incorporate women into mainstream theoretical perspectives on aging is a reflection of resistance to incorporating women into society and hence into sociological research.

"Mainstream" here refers to dominant theories in the sociological field, such as functionalist and political economy of old age theories, whose proponents could be accused of being "gender blind." As Arber and Ginn (1995) point out, there exists a tiny handful of feminist writers who take the topic of age seriously in understanding gender.

According to Acker (1988, cited in Arber and Ginn 1991), in all known societies the relations of distribution and production are influenced by gender and thus take on a gendered meaning. Gender relations of distribution in capitalist society are historically rooted and are transformed as the means of production change. Similarly, age relations are linked to the capitalist mode of production and relations of distribution. "Wages" take on a specific meaning depending on age. For example, teenagers work for less money than adults, who in turn work for less money than middle-aged adults. Further, young children rely on personal relations with family figures such as parents. Many older people rely on resources distributed by the state.

Introduction 15

Older women are viewed as unworthy of respect or consideration (Arber and Ginn 1991). Catherine Itzin claims the double standard of aging arises from sets of conventional expectations as to age-pertinent attitudes and roles for each sex, which apply in patriarchal society. These are defined by Itzin as a male and a female "chronology," socially defined and sanctioned so that the experience of prescribed roles is sanctioned by disapproval. Male chronology hinges on employment, but a woman's age status is defined in terms of events in the reproductive cycle (Itzin 1986).

It is perhaps emblematic of contemporary Western society that aging marginalizes the experiences of women through an interconnected oppression of gender and aging. The reason for this, as Arber and Ginn (1991) claim, is that patriarchal society exercises power through the chronologies of employment and reproduction, and through the sexualized promotion of a "youthful" appearance in women. This has been shown to be correct in terms of job segregation, marginalization, powerlessness, and the "double jeopardy" of being a woman and being old. Arguably, Arber and Ginn (1991, 1995) maintain that, because women's value is exercised, the awareness of a loss of a youthful appearance brings social devaluation; vulnerability to pressure is penetrated by cosmeticization. Indeed, the "beauty industrial complex" makes huge profits by articulating "anti-aging" creams and other products. It is estimated that L'Oreal has an annual turnover of $9.4 billion on anti-aging products (Powell 2002). Further, Mary Daly (cited in Arber and Ginn 1991) draws a mirror image between Western cosmetic surgery and the genital mutilation carried out in some African societies: both cultured practices demonstrate the pressure on women to comply with male standards of desirability and the extent of male domination. For older black women, the ideal of "beauty" portrayed by white male culture was doubly distant and alienating, until growing black consciousness subverted disparaging language and argued "black is beautiful" through resistance to patriarchal and racist power relations.

Gender and Marginality in Old Age

In the United States, women comprise 59 percent of those over sixty-five; they account for 72 percent of the older poor (Powell 2001b). According to Estes and Associates (2001), the poverty rate in the United States is 19 percent, of which older women are the poorest social group. In 1993 older women's average income was 43 percent lower than that of older men. Poorest of all are older black women, with 82 percent classified as poor or "near poor." Indeed, for many women, such negative financial conditions would express powerlessness and economic marginalization. Many older women's adverse financial situations came about because their participation in the labor market was limited and dominated by men, thus generating "dependency" upon men. In terms of social security benefits, 66 percent of older women received benefits below the poverty line. Further, the work of Janet Finch (1986) has problematized the construction of social services in Western society for poorer older women by describing how such services contribute to dominant discursive constructions of older women as "incapable" and "dependent."

While feminist theorizing in gerontology continues to raise important questions relating to aging and gender, there are other identity variables that are still given scant attention, a problem that is replicated across functionalism, critical gerontology, and feminist modern theories. In order to address this, the next section explores two issues—race and sexuality—which are important to consider if the full complexity of the processes surrounding modernist discourses of aging are to be understood and appreciated.

RACE AND AGING

According to Powell and Longino (2002) issues of ethnicity in social gerontology have been scarcely researched. First, social gerontology could highlight the significance of cultural values, ethnic traditions, and a sense of belonging to a group with shared experiences in which older individuals may

Introduction   17

ground their identities. Second, the experience of older black people of being a minority within a minority is important. An examination of the minority concept raises questions about the validity of supposed majority "white" norms. Third, the experiences of minority ethnic groups in trying to obtain social justice and fairness in terms of health care, for example, expose the ethnocentrist nature of social welfare in Western culture.

Boneham and Blakemore (1994) claim that the dominant theories of age and aging need to be reconsidered with racial diversity in mind. Such views of macrotheories of functionalism, political economy, and feminism have ignored the experiences of older black people (Patel 1990).

Further, the biomedical model has discussed how the aging body has declined and has attempted to discover variations through different explanations of the body in different cultures. For example, Stuart Hall (1992) has considered how scientific definitions of "race" are racist and somehow attempt to explain physical characteristics of people and behaviors. Compounding the decline model with inferior/superior scientific discourses generates what Sim (1990) has called "metaphors of pathology," which seep into Western society to engender what Hall (1992) calls different "historical forms of racisms." According to Hall (1992), racism in Western culture is linked with colonialism and slavery, legacies of the history of the Enlightenment and industrial capitalism in the U.K., United States, and Europe. Conceptually, the concept of "race" refers to a "category composed of individuals who share biologically transmitted traits that members of a society deem socially significant" (Saraga 1998, 324). A critical perspective goes underneath the surface to raise critical questions about categories or types of people based on classification. "Racism" refers to the idea that one racial category is innately superior or inferior to another. Therefore, the assertion of one specific category of individuals over others has served as a powerful tool for relegating the targets of taunts to a status of social inferiority.

According to Patel (1990) the "economic and social conditions of older black people can be explained away by 'blaming the victim.' The focus on such arguments then shifts from individual pathology to family deficiency to cultural defects."

Indeed, Simon Biggs (1993) claims the myth of "looking after one's own" is replicated by professional and institutional practices and services. Biggs (1993) sees the deficiencies in the system that are at fault but the "passing of the buck" by the system is to pathologize stereotypical views that "it's their fault" if they do not provide for their own.

The assumption that ethnic communities are made up entirely of caring, close-knit, extended families that do not require outside care and support has meant that the state, both local and central, has failed to meet the needs of population groups that run along ethnic lines. For example, despite the growing proportion of older black people, very few attend local day care centers or residential care. They are often put off, partly by the absence of other black service users and by the predominance of Western ideologies and traditions regarding activities and fare (Bond and Coleman 1990). Similarly, Wing Au (1996, cited in Powell 2001b) found that among the older Chinese community in Liverpool, Great Britain, social service departments were very slow to meet their care needs because they thought "they looked after their own." This highlights a restricted view of culture in which the concept of normalization causes the system to overlook the very people whom social services should be treating.

Open racism continues to exist. Hall (1992) claims that black older people are subjected to racist abuse and experienced hostility from white older people. Patel (1990, 39) claims that "sufficient importance may not be attached to instances of racial abuse in a home because staff involved deem it as insignificant or because white elders cannot be expected to change their behaviour. Hence black elders must put up with racism or not use the service." Indeed, according to Alcock (1996), there exists institutional racism in the British National Health Service in that older black people are not treated by medical staff, including nurses and doctors, the same as older white people. Indeed, not only are there serious questions about health disadvantages coupled with this, but also the manifestation of "elder abuse" is not detected and consequently many older black people do not have their concerns, needs, or situations addressed. Furthermore, Boneham and Blakemore (1994) suggest that the problems faced by older men and women from both Asian and Afro-Caribbean communities are posed in terms of the

Introduction 19

devaluation of old age in Western culture, based on consumer demand and reflecting racial disadvantage by a lack of adequate social facilities.

Culture itself can be silencing for many older black people. Hazan (1980, cited in Boneham and Blakemore 1994) compiled a study of an older Jewish community and found that many older people found it painful to talk about memories of the past such as the Holocaust but were dismissed by white professional health workers who had no comparable experience, which in turn created distrust and anxiety.

SEXUALITY AND AGING

The issue of sexuality has been marginal to modernist theories of aging. The oldest gay men and lesbians have few, if any, positive role models for coupling, aging, or creating alternative family structures (Isay 1996; Fullmer 1995). Fullmer explains that people "coming out" later in life must integrate themselves into a new culture and may be faced with some of the same tasks that typically confront adolescents and young adults, and that the age of coming out could influence family structure and support systems. This indicates that the later in life a person comes out, the more difficult it is to integrate into a gay/lesbian social network or restructure the family system one is in to allow for the gay/lesbian relationship (Isay 1996). Fullmer remarks that now that more gay and lesbian couples have the opportunity to adopt children, they may have children and grandchildren who may be more accepting of them and are there to support them in their old age. Gay men or lesbians who have gone from a heterosexual relationship to a homosexual one might encounter more problems with their biological children accepting their sexuality at a time when they may need them the most (Saraga 1998).

Families of older gay and lesbian people have many of the same strengths and deal with the same issues as other families. But along with getting older, they also have to face the prejudices of being gay or lesbian (Fullmer 1995). "Older gays and lesbians have learned through a lifetime of experience that they will likely be discriminated against if it is known that they are homosexual. It is common in our society to typify older gay men and lesbians as pathetic and lonely 'dirty old men' or 'child molesters,' as 'old maids' or as 'drag queens'" (Fullmer 1995, 66). Gay and lesbian couples and their families may be alienated from institutions such as churches because many religious organizations have been very vocal in their condemnation of homosexuality (Fullmer 1995).

Public retirement housing does not allow "unrelated adults" to live under the same roof. This includes nursing homes and private retirement centers, which can make assumptions that their residents are heterosexual and structure activities on the basis of these assumptions (Isay 1996). Hospitals often have policies that allow only "immediate" family members to be in the rooms of seriously ill patients and help make decisions for them. It is also not uncommon for biological family members to contest a will that names a homosexual partner as the beneficiary and win, because there is no legally defined relationship between the partners (Dalley 1988).

The major sociological issue and lesson to be learned here is how to overcome the impact of class, race, and gender without merely adding more identity formations, such as race and sexuality, to the task of understanding aging in modernity.

Taken together, different yet modernist theories of aging consisting of functionalism, critical gerontology, and feminist gerontology have helped shape important debates about the extent and nature of an "aging" society. Such social theories have been used also to analyze pressing social issues such as the engagement of older people with society, active aging, pension politics, and the gendered nature of aging in modernity. However, the concerns of these theoretical resources have been primarily macro-oriented: for example, the political economy approach overemphasizes structural disadvantage (cf. Walker 1985) or "structured dependency" (Townsend 1981) at the expense of focus to older people's sense of human agency in, for example, fighting for political and economic representation through social organization (Tulle 2004).

Such modernist models of aging, by focusing upon the social problems of older people, may have taken up, promoted, and reinforced the "ageism" which many are arguing against (Bytheway 1995). Consequently, modernist epistemologies of aging can be regarded as over-arching explanations of

Introduction 21

aging. Thus one finds diversity, subjectivity, and microdimensions of aging in the lifestyles and experiences of older people.

Indeed, a pressing question may be, what makes such theories modernist? They are modernist in the sense that they have afforded "grand narratives" to aging. For example, they supply macrogeneralizations to their area of social concern: "in the interests of capitalism" and "in the interests of patriarchy." For Powell and Longino (2002) an alternative form of theorizing drawn from postmodernism suggests that "grand theories" place too many limits on what is conceptually possible regarding aging and that it is too totalized. The objectification of older people that is implied by the term "social class" and "gender" relegates individuals to socially constructed categories. Likewise, the Marxist notion of "false consciousness" fails to recognize that this can be patronizing to many people who resist social marginalization. For Featherstone and Hepworth (1993), individual experiences are no longer believed to be determined by such social constructs such as "class." A postmodern perspective has tended to take a critical stance relative to Marxist developments. It attempts instead to tease out ontologically flexible depictions of aging, and it questions the truth of claims behind ontological and epistemological generalizations based on "concrete" social divisions such as race, class, and gender, which are touchstones of modern gerontological theories (Biggs 1999).

The next chapter focuses on postmodern constructions of aging that alternatively emphasize the cultural interaction between the aging body and social context in shaping the way people experience their lifetimes. Even though lives are seen as embedded in social relationships, popular culture, and history, the notion of the "aging body" is an important narrative in the social construction of aging identity. This view has rich epistemological and ontological implications in terms of understanding the aging self and social reality. It draws upon attempts to overcome the aging body as articulated by biomedical gerontology. In terms of identity, we are talking about the possibilities of reinvention and denial of limits. In many ways this approach also reflects the "outside-looking-in" perspective insofar as, as social theory, aging is bounded by the internal-external duality and the possibilities that the external makes available. The reterritorialization of the aging body by society, and paradigmatically by postmodern social theory, is a strategy that parallels the denial of subjectivity within the main traditions of the biomedical model.

Chapter 2

THEORIZING EMBODIMENT, POSTMODERNISM AND AGING

In the previous chapter we interrogated the social construction of aging and old age comprising of mainstream theories of functionalism, political economy of old age, and feminist gerontology, which maintained that aging is reduced to disengagement/activity and social roles and affected not only by capitalism and economic forces but also by patriarchy and the exploitation of all women by men. It can be suggested that such mainstream theories, by focusing on the bigger picture of life, exclude social relations at the micro texture of everyday life. This is not to deny the important and critical points that have been made by the sociological theories discussed in the previous chapter. Indeed, such approaches are significant to pointing to emergence of social problems of aging as cast through the socioeconomic gaze.

Notwithstanding this, and despite the consolidation of these important theories of aging, there was no specific innovative theoretical development with a specific focus on an understanding of the "body." Although functionalism and political economy have their theoretical differences, they both focused on structures to the exclusion of the body. The contentious point to make here is that, by ignoring the sense of "lived experiences" of older people, all modernist theories provide perceptions of adult aging that are over generalized.

Understanding aging bodies plays a crucial part in the identity formation of older people in the representations of the body. Outside of gerontology, feminism has focused on the ways younger women's bodies were controlled and dominated within patriarchy. According to Twigg (2000), feminism has focused our attention as to how women represent the body itself. The current interest in the body and embodiment in social and human sciences encompasses a range of themes and theoretical traditions (Powell 2001c). Historically, the discipline of sociology ignored the centrality of the body in terms of its prioritized "rational" or scientific analysis of modern social systems (Oberg and Tornstam 1999; Wahidin and Powell 2001). Indeed, the sociological tradition has focused upon the social forces that impinge upon the construction of personal biographies and the society in which sociologists live (Mills 1959). The sociological aspirations of Karl Marx, Emile Durkheim, and Max Weber distanced them from a study of the body in order to generate intellectual respectability to ideas about social order and social change (Turner 1989). Sociology simultaneously distanced itself from biological reductionism, which, as part of the "project of modernity," attempted to talk of the body as an object to be predicted and controlled. Coupled with this, the modernist preoccupation with theorizing and constructing grand narratives in theories of aging has also tended to exclude an analysis of the body. As Powell (2001b) points out, theorizing occupies a commanding position in sociological analysis; with a preoccupation with abstraction, bodies are things to be transcended or ignored.

Moreover, gerontology continues to be in the thrall of a biomedical discourse on aging (Powell and Longino 2001); although concerned with the fixed limitations of the aging body, it restricts an ontologically flexible understanding of aging. Conversely, we can question how the aging body acquires meaning, and also how the meaningful body itself, in its turn, influences and limits signifying processes and social efforts as related to society and culture.

The central focus is not on the body as a natural given, or as the conglomerate of neurons, hormones, and genes, but rather as a concrete

Theorizing Embodiment, Postmodernism and Aging 25

social and cultural practice of everyday life. Traditionally, the body in its actual realities has been generally neglected within the social sciences and humanities (Shilling 1993; Katz 1996). The investigation of the body was more or less relegated to biology and the medical sciences. In recent years, however, the body has made a major comeback within all realms of scholarly and scientific research (Shilling 1993). Especially those fields that have traditionally focused on the "inanimate" aspects of reality. For example, literary critics, film theorists, political scientists, historians have shown an upsurge in interest in a variety of "bodily matters." That is, in the concrete, corporeal dimensions which render us all recognizable human beings, the physical aspects of our individual and collective embodied specificity and experiences.

It is by querying the role of the body that one can move away from the modernist biomedical approach, which locates the body within the naturalistic framework (Powell and Longino 2001). The postmodern perspective adds a richness to the literature by examining embodiment and the corporeality of the body in all its social guises (Wahidin and Powell 2001, 2003). It places the body not as a passive materiality that is acted upon but one that negotiates the capillaries of power, enabling itself to be always in the process of becoming through the experiences of embodiment (Longino and Powell 2004). Moreover, in a postmodern culture, the prospect of an endless life has been revived through consumer images of perpetual youth and the blurring of traditional life-course boundaries (Featherstone and Hepworth 1993).

Therefore, this chapter focuses on such themes as conceptualizing postmodernism, theorizing the aging body, popular culture and aging body; gendered bodies, and finally biotechnologies and the reconstruction of aging bodies.

THE DEVELOPMENT OF POSTMODERN SOCIAL THEORY

The theory of postmodernism represents a decisive break with modernity (Delanty 1999; Powell and Longino 2002). Postmodernism emerged from Western social theory; the debate was instigated by Derrida, Baudrillard, and Lyotard in the tradition of the modern and calls for breaks within this tradition. This is clearly illustrated by the work of French postmodern theorist Baudrillard, who adopted an extreme abandonment of Enlightenment values in his devastating critique of modernist approaches in sociology. Baudrillard focuses on the transcendental nature of society through the concept of hyperreality. He argued that in modern society there is no distinction between reality and illusion (Seidman 1994; May 1996) and that individuals live their lives through a simulation of reality. Nothing has any true origin or authenticity, and lived experience is itself a mere construction, made of a series of depthless signs and representations (Smart 1993, 52). In this way Baudrillard argues that sociology can no longer serve a political purpose, because power relations have been dispersed through the hyperreal nature of society (Smart 1993, 55). The "neat divisions," "hierarchies," and "foundational premises" of both modernity and sociology (Seidman 1994, 347) are no longer relevant. In particular, Baudrillard rejects the economic determinism of Marxism and states that there are no longer such fundamental systems of exploitation, only superficial simulations and exchanges (May 1996):

> Like the philosopher Nietzsche, Baudrillard criticizes such claims to truth and favours a model based on what he calls seduction. Seduction plays on the surface: it is the surface appearance that is effective in determining action, not some latent or hidden structure as claimed by Marxism or Freudianism. (Thompson 1992, 244)

For Lyotard (1984) the project of modernity has become obsolete and society had entered the "postmodern condition." Lyotard deconstructs the way in which bodies of knowledge are created in order to legitimate hierarchical structures in society. In his influential work *The Postmodern Condition* (1984, first published in French in 1979), Lyotard looked at the changes that have occurred to the nature of "knowledge" throughout history. He pointed to how premodern society was based on narratives that were made up of religion and myth (Seidman 1994, 206). Knowledge was a body

Theorizing Embodiment, Postmodernism and Aging 27

of stories that were thought to explain the way society was and determine that which was "good" or "evil." In this way such narratives legitimated the social rules of behavior that determined how society was structured and who had authority (Seidman 1994, 206). In contrast, modernity, Lyotard argued, was thought to be based on "true" knowledge that rejected the "narratives" of premodernity. However, in *The Postmodern Condition*, Lyotard asserts that in actual fact supposedly "pure," "real" scientific knowledge is also self-legitimating, so is itself merely another "narrative" (McLennan 1992, 332). Lyotard argues that scientific thought and knowledge have political and philosophical agendas and are therefore value laden and not totally objective (McLennan 1992, 333). An ideal that underpinned the beginnings of Enlightenment thought was that the attainment of absolute knowledge for all would mean the attainment of absolute freedom for all (May 1996).

It was thought that knowledge was the key to breaking down power structures that had existed during the domination of premodern narratives. But Lyotard pointed to the contradictions within modern scientific bodies of knowledge and argued that they are themselves still made up of hierarchical power structures. Just as in earlier societies narratives served to determine who had the right to speak and who did not, Lyotard states, this is still the case. Hierarchies still operate and serve to give the decision-making elite the power to decide what gets defined as legitimate knowledge.

> Countless scientists have seen their "move" ignored or repressed, sometimes for decades, because it too abruptly destabilized the accepted positions, not only in the university and scientific hierarchy, but also in the problematic. (Lyotard 1984, 63)

Lyotard argues, therefore, that science can no longer be seen as a unified body working toward the emancipation of humanity (Longino and Powell 2004). His ideas can be linked to those of Nietzsche, who believes that "truth" and "knowledge" are merely a matter of conventions that falsify and dissimulate to promote human survival (May 1996). Rather than being a grand quest for universal laws, Lyotard argues, knowledge is sought in order to keep human society functioning efficiently (Steuerman 1992, 108). The

28 *Jason L. Powell and Sheying Chen*

assertion by science that it is constantly objectively striving for truth and progress is called into question by the fact that the search for knowledge is inextricably linked to achieving economic growth in society (McLennan 1992, 332). That is not to say that these two things are incompatible, but rather to question if the search for truth and progress can ever be totally objective when there is a financial incentive. Lyotard argues that those involved in striving for progress "allocate our lives for the growth of power. In matters of social justice and of scientific truth alike, the legitimation of that power is based on its optimizing the system's performance—efficiency" (Lyotard 1984, xxiv).

Since, as Lyotard (1984) points out, the legitimation of science can be called into question, knowledge as a unified, overarching metanarrative (such as the Enlightenment narrative that knowledge equals liberation, as was key in modernity) breaks down into a wide range of "micronarratives" (Lyotard 1984, xxiv). Each separate specialism has a different discourse and plays different "language games" in an attempt to gain accreditation from its specific audience (Seidman 1994, 208; Lyotard 1984, 64). This, to Lyotard is what ultimately characterizes the postmodern condition.

Lyotard's rejection of grand narratives obviously has strong implications for the structure of social gerontology. By rejecting the belief in the ability to universalize, philosophical thought loses its authority to make any suggestions as to what action can be taken in order to make changes in society (Smart 1993, 37). In response to the criticisms of the Enlightenment made by Lyotard, Habermas wishes to consolidate the "project of modernity" and further argues that we should not completely abandon the possibility of a rational pursuit of truth (Steuerman 1992, 107). He defends modernity and argues that what is needed is more philosophical discussion, not less (Steuerman 1992, 113). Habermas states that through the use of communicative action, language, and rational dialogue, the Enlightenment aims of truth, justice, and freedom are still attainable alongside social consensus (Steuerman 1992, 104–7). However, Lyotard argues that Habermas ignores the fact that communication cannot simply take the form of consensual, rational dialogue; it will always take place in the context of power struggles (Powell and Biggs 2000).

Theorizing Embodiment, Postmodernism and Aging

Therefore, rather than holding on to the ideals of Enlightenment scientific thought, Lyotard might suggest that we attempt to "restructure" social theory (and social gerontology) in a postmodern vein so that we might find a democratic, pluralistic solution (Seidman 1994, 207). He argued that while grand narratives, such as the Marxian narrative of class conflict, were well intentioned and essential to modernist social theory, to continue to utilize such concepts fails adequately to challenge the hierarchical structures in society and therefore continues to marginalize and repress issues of difference.

"Postmodernism abandons absolute standards, universal categories and grand theories in favour of local, contextualized, and pragmatic conceptual strategies" (Seidman 1994, 207). Seidman outlines the postmodern idea that the splintering of metanarratives has occurred to such an extent that society has become decentered. That is, there is no longer a common unifying culture in existence (Seidman 1994, 206). Individuals experience their lives at constantly shifting intersections of different discourses and language games. Instances of oppression, therefore, occur in many different contexts as individuals constantly construct, deconstruct, and reconstruct themselves in terms of these "fractured identities" (Powell 2000). Indeed, Lyotard argues that a postmodern analysis does offer a way of explaining issues of multiplicity and difference (Lyotard 1984, 81).

Powell and Longino (2002) suggest that there are several themes that are shared in postmodern analysis of aging, which consolidate Baudrillard's, Lyotard's and Seidman's theoretical excursions. First, there is distrust in the concept of absolute and objective truth. "Truth" is viewed as contextual, situational, and conditional (Biggs and Powell 2001). Second, emphasis is placed on fragmentation rather than universalism, again pushing away from the general and toward the particular (Powell 2001b). Third, local power is preferred over the centralized power of the nation-state, and decentralization, or the process of democratization of power, is a pervasive theme of postmodern narratives (Powell and Longino 2001). Fourth, reality is simulated but is otherwise not held to be a very meaningful concept; reality conceived as a general and universal truth is profoundly doubted (Powell and Longino 2002). Fifth, we are seeing the rise and consolidation of consumer culture that tends to put "power" in the hands of the consumers but can also equally manipulate consumers through marketing ploys and interpolating discourses of consumer freedom by dictating costs in the global marketplace (Biggs and Powell 2001). Finally, diversity and difference are emphasized and valued above commonality based on homogeneity (Powell 2001b; May 1996). Postmodern analysis of culture is no longer a fringe perspective inasmuch as it apparently promotes strategies of individualism and diversity, and postmodernism is critical of strategies that devalue individuals because of any characteristic that would control access to knowledge and could thereby assault identity (Biggs and Powell 2001). In ethics, as in epistemology, the final result is a kind of moral relativism (Longino and Powell 2004).

Central to postmodern assertions is that in the twenty-first century there has occurred a radical shift in the constitution of social order, paralleling the significance of the Enlightenment and birth of modernity that led to the emergence of the biomedical sciences and social sciences in general. This new sociocultural formation has been termed postmodernity and is seen as to be characterized by increasing diversity and the loosening of structural modernist principles. Postmodern thought may be seen as a revolt against both the structural version of gerontology theory, that is political economy and feminism, and as a break with the rigidity and certainties of the positivist or biomedical strand of gerontology. All forms of meaning and "knowledge" are rendered problematic and no longer to be taken for granted as the myth of the biomedical objectivity is debunked. Hence, the controversial point is that modernist sociological theories claim the same forms of certainty, universalism, and rigidity that are seen as master narratives of positivism. For example, political economy of aging (cf. Estes 1979) emphasizes the importance of economic materiality, applicable to every older person in North America. But this has also been conflated with the biomedical obsession with an objective social world that was to be scientifically knowable. Although the political foundations of these very two different "modernist" explanations are diametrically opposed, they are treated as one in treating aging as an "object" to be predicted or problematized.

Theorizing Embodiment, Postmodernism and Aging

Postmodern discussions relating to the aging body in social gerontology are slowly developing (Powell and Longino 2002). While the "body" as a concept implies an objectified and "natural" entity, the body is now beginning to be viewed as increasingly complex. The importance of the body to gerontology is in many ways obvious. For example, illness can limit the "normal" functioning of the body, and this can have profound psychological, political, and social consequences that interest gerontologists of all backgrounds. Moreover, health is often thought of in terms of body maintenance, and such activities form a pivotal feature of consumer societies. However at a personal level the age one appears to be may be different from the age one actually is, as though one is wearing a disguise. Featherstone and Hepworth (1993) maintain that old age is a mask that "conceals the essential identity of the person beneath" (148). That is, while the external appearance is changing with age, the essential identity is not, so that the difference between physical appearance and the unchanging image in his or her head may surprise the aging individual. Bytheway and Johnson (1998) assert that we need a well-constituted image of what "old" looks like before we could recognize the signs in our own images. Thompson (1992) argues that people derive their sense of identity in later life from the achievements of the past and what remains to be accomplished in the future, rather than from a set of stereotypical, usually negative, attributes of old age. Unless they are ill or depressed, old people do not feel old "inside." Furthermore, old people tend to associate old age with the residents of nursing homes, an image from which they want to distance themselves (Biggs 1999).

Simultaneously, the aging body has been exploited by popular consumer culture, which has attempted to colonize narratives afforded to the aging body (Longino and Powell 2004). Morris (1998) agrees, asserting that consumer culture is preoccupied with reconstructing aging bodies, promoted through the glamorized representations of advertising. The visual image is increasingly dominant in Western culture; images can also be used to disseminate alternative constructions of old age. In their analysis of retirement magazines, Featherstone and Hepworth (1993) argue that the types of images of old people presented in specialist magazines are consonant with attempts at focusing on the positive side of being old. This is usually linked to "young" old age, early retirement, and the continuation of full activities, usually through the engagement in leisure activities funded by careful financial planning. The message here is that there now exist opportunities for consumption (McAdams 1993; Gilleard and Higgs 2000) and enjoyment in old age that act as a counterpoint to traditional images of old people inexorably driven toward death via senility, physical decrepitude, loneliness, and disengagement. Thus, consumer society reinforces negative language and images of later life; in turn, this can produce a slide into "symbolic" death (Powell and Longino 2001).

Indeed, postmodern gerontology would claim that life-course models that associate aging with both decline and universal stages of life are fundamentally flawed (Powell and Longino 2001). To exemplify the fluid and blurred nature of aging identity, a uni-age style, Meyrowitz (1984, cited in Featherstone and Hepworth 1993), argues that in Western society, "children" are becoming more like adults and adults more childlike. There is a growing similarity in modes of presentation of self, gestures and postures, fashions, and leisure-time pursuits adopted by both parents and their children.

For Featherstone and Hepworth (1993) the private sphere of family life is becoming less private, as children are granted access to the larger world through popular media such as television and the Internet. Previously concealed aspects of adult life (such as sex, death, money, and problems besetting adults who are anxious about the roles and selves they present to children) are no longer so easy to keep secret. A uni-age behavioral style is influenced by the advent of media imagery that, as a powerful form of communication, bypasses the controls that adults once established over the kinds of information believed to be suitable for children. (An interesting premodern comparison relative to childhood resides with the work of Aries. He claims that in premodern times the child was allowed to participate as an adult after the age of seven.). One contribution of postmodern ideas is to illuminate the blurring of age identities in terms of "dress" and "work."

Therefore, the importance of the "body" to social gerontology is in many ways apparent. For example, the body in pain: illness can limit functions of

Theorizing Embodiment, Postmodernism and Aging 33

the body and have effects that attract the interest of social gerontologists of all backgrounds globally. David B. Morris posits in his engaging study, *The Culture of Pain*: "Pain not only hurts but more often than not frustrates, baffles, and resists us. Yet it seems we cannot simply suffer pain but most always are compelled to make sense of it" (Morris 1991, 18).

Beyond the problem of making sense of pain (for example), the reason why the body is central to the discipline of social gerontology is that the biomedical model in particular has given intellectual respectability to "scientific" ideas concerning aging that raise issues about altering the boundaries of the physical body (Freund 1988). For example, biomedical science can reconstruct bodies through plastic surgery. Further, it can interfere with genetic structures; and it can swap internal organs from one human body to another (Haraway 1991; Powell and Longino 2001). "We," according to Haraway (1991), have become "cyborgs"—not wholly machines and not wholly natural organisms either. She argues: "Twentieth century machines have made thoroughly ambiguous the difference between natural and artificial, mind and body, self-developing and externally designed, and many other distinctions that used to apply to organisms and machines" (10).

However, Shilling (1993) argues that there is a schizophrenic ambivalence about the body: the more we know about bodies, and the more we are able to control, intervene, and restructure them, the more uncertain we become as to what the body really is. The boundaries between the physical body and society are becoming increasingly bifurcated. The body, like parchment, is written upon, inscribed by variables such as gender, age, sexual orientation, and ethnicity and by a series of inscriptions that are dependent on types of spaces and places. However, as Shilling (1993) powerfully argues, the more we know about bodies, the more we are able to govern and modify norms: highlighting how gendered and ageist discourses serve to confine and define aging bodies.

The role of the body has become a discursive site of power to be produced, acted upon, and received. Sandra Bartky, for instance, has argued that "normative femininity is coming more and more to be centred on woman's body. Not its duties and obligations or even its capacity to bear children, but its sexuality, more precisely its presumed heterosexuality and its appearance" (S. Bartky 1988, quoted in Wahidin and Powell 2003, 8).

One cannot argue in relation to body modification that the performance of the body is solely one to counter hegemonic biomedical discourses, or one based purely on aesthetic value, without fully encapsulating the varied and multifaceted technologies of the corporeal and the self. Through these bodily practices, old bodies are transforming their gendered habitus and thus creating identities for themselves that transgress the boundaries of how to manage old bodies (Longino and Powell 2004).

Bryan S. Turner (1995) emphasizes several key processes that work upon and within the body across time and space. Longino and Powell (2004) give as an example, here, how the effort to crack the genetic code of biological aging has directed attention away from socially determined life-chances in later life. Power relations become eclipsed by narratives of technological application subject to manipulation and control by a skilled professional. This is often a concern of medical students as they begin their education, but it is also often lost as part of their induction into a biomedical culture (Longino and Powell 2004).

Powell and Longino (2002) have argued that the disaggregation of the aging body takes a number of forms. First, the experience of aging is broken down into a number of separate age categories, each with its accompanying medical specialism. Second, the dominance of biomedical perspectives on aging has led to an acceptance of the association between adult aging and bodily and mental deterioration. Finally they note that a combination of specialism and a separation of mind from the body has compromised the gendered experience of bodily aging (Powell and Longino 2002). If aging becomes associated with illness, and the avoidance of aging with cure, then an expansion of medical discourse to include ever more aspects of the older person's life-world leaves two alternatives: subsumption of the self under the rubric of a sick body or a continual flight from the "symptoms" of aging (Longino and Powell 2004). Both depend upon biomedical hegemony (Biggs and Powell 2001). It follows from the above analysis that a biomedical approach to aging encourages the evacuation of certain forms of

Theorizing Embodiment, Postmodernism and Aging

experience through the reclassification of experience into symptoms that can then be addressed separately from wider social impacts (Phillipson 1998).

Frank (1998) argues that the ability to tell one's own story of illness is by no means straightforward. If, as Foucault (1977) claims, the maintenance of existing power relations depends not on the use of force but on the ability to persuade active subjects to reproduce those relations for themselves, then the telling of narratives will always be suspect. Further, Frank (1996) poses the almost unanswerable question, when does self-care turn into a technology for producing a certain sort of self? For example, Estes, Biggs, and Phillipson (2003) suggest that personal narratives, particularly for older people in health settings, remain both a means of taking care of oneself and conformity to a restricted legitimizing discourse of their bodies and physical appearance.

Simultaneously, becoming, and being, old are about the corporeality of being old, the experience of holding on to physical/mental integrity and reasonable health (Baltes and Carstersen 1996). It is therefore important to focus on the construction of identity that is imposed upon the discourses of exteriority and interiority that impinge upon the body.

The postmodern interest in the body presents paradoxical aspects of the contemporary world. On the one hand, is obsessed by the body and its materiality, emphasized by the attention given over to it in the media and consumer society in general; on the other hand, it has emptied the body of its symbolic meaning. It is no coincidence that recent artistic performances (e.g., body art) and popular youth culture practices (e.g., body piercing) appear like a desperate and contradictory attempt to recover the ritual significance of the body. To examine historically the various theories about the body is to become aware that Western culture has always, in a Manichean manner, separated the material from the spiritual, the body from the soul (May 1996). Western philosophy, founded on the Platonic dichotomy between body and soul, has considered the body as a prison and tomb for the psyche. Intellect in the Platonic conception becomes an autonomous and independent entity (May 1996). This disjoining operation conceived the soul positively and the body, with its materiality, negatively. As May (1996) stresses, this paradox in Western culture is to be found at the origin of Greek civilization because, if philosophical thought tries to disregard the body because of its corporeality, it nevertheless returns as a metaphor for the representation of the political system. In place of this dichotomy, primitive communities have endowed the body with a polysemic meaning: the body was the center of a symbolic network that ensured that both the natural and social world were modeled on its possibilities. In this way, the body was never an isolated and single entity but always a cosmic one, part of a community. Every individual managed to preserve, by means of a dense circulation of symbols connecting the one with the whole, his/her own individual perception of the body, albeit within a range of multiplicities and differences. At a time when youthfulness is valued, the dislocation felt between the eternality of the body or the surfaces of the body that symbolize the self and the internality of the body leaves many to combat age through "maintaining" their bodies via the commodification of youth.

The performance of the body is indicative of how the body is a discursive site of power to be produced, acted upon, negotiated, and received. These techniques create the space for resistance, enabling power to be positive yet at the same time negative. It is the polysemic nature of the body in all its guises that the performance is not solely one to counter, resist, and subvert hegemonic biomedical discourses. It is rather a relationship encapsulating the multivaried technologies of corporeal and self inscriptions based on what went on before, the present and immediate past (Wahidin and Powell 2003).

In a postmodern culture, the prospect of an endless life has been revived through consumer images of perpetual youth and a blurring of traditional life-course boundaries (Featherstone and Hepworth 1993). Bauman (1992) posits of the "postmodern strategy of survival," compared to "traditional ways of dabbling with timelessness," that: "instead of trying (in vain) to colonize the future, it dissolves it in the present. It does not allow the finality of time to worry the living ... by oscillating time (all of it, exhaustively, without residue) into short lived, evanescent episodes. It rehearses mortality, so to speak, by practicing it day by day" (Bauman 1992, 2).

POPULAR CULTURE AND THE AGING BODY

Throughout particular literary texts and through representations of the celebrated youthful body, the old body is something to be feared and resisted and thus at all costs should be held at bay (Longino and Powell 2004; Powell and Longino 2002).

For example, the motif of the woman's body transposed into a mythical and allegorical dimension returns in an essay on Irish women's literature in which Roberta Gefter Wondrich examines the contradictory relationship that women have with the images related to the myth of Ireland as a nation. On the one hand, Ireland is a great mother, a Marian Catholic image characterized by self-denial, an ever obedient woman who sacrifices herself for her son and is thus essentially passive; on the other hand, Ireland is the "old woman" who symbolizes the nation devastated by its destroyers (Greenblatt 1980).

The sense of isolation marks the works of a writer like Samuel Beckett, who uses the elderly body to express the absurdity of existence (Miller 1993). In several of his plays, Beckett represented old age through the violent divide between body and mind; he dramatized the inevitable physical decay of the body, until the only trace left of it on the stage is the word, the voice. Beckett studied and explored all the possible relations between the elderly body and space, between body and movement and between body and the objects that surround it. Beckett's ideal seems to be that of a man on a bicycle, a sort of a Cartesian centaur who emblematizes the phrase "mens sana in corpore disposito." In this respect the author explodes the dilemma "Cogito ergo sum": he rebels against the definition of man as a thinking machine (Miller 1993). Beckett's characters experience a tension between mind and body: a mind that is subject to continuous changes even if imprisoned in a body that is caught in a process of decaying and decrepitude. It is interesting to compare Beckett's characters with the disconcerting images of painter Francis Bacon, which are characterized by a prevailing sense of the vulnerability of man and, above all, his solitude, in the hell of the modern condition (Miller 1993). At the center of Bacon's representation is a view of man as a contingency, a creature with a disfigured face and body.

This can be seen in his *Study after Velazquez's Portrait of Pope Innocent X* (1953), in which the theme of the cage and the imprisonment of the body underlines the horror of old age, emphasized by the screaming mouth of the figure (Greenblatt 1980).

Powell and Longino (2002) deal with some paradoxes implicit in our postmodern society, which is characterized by global information networks that work to project a conformist and consumerist view of the body and, at the same time, testifies to the different perceptions of the body by heterogeneous ethnic groups and peoples. The recent information revolution has forced us once again to question the relationship between the body and the machine. If it is true that the continuous bombardment of television images of mutilated and cut-up bodies has, so to speak, dematerialized them, on the other hand, the corporeality of the body comes obsessively back, as mentioned earlier, in the tribal rites that young people in the big metropolises impress on themselves.

Longino and Powell (2004, 177) further suggest that the aging body has a negative representation by cartoon fiction:

> Cartoonists tend to include deep lines on the face and loose skin beneath the chin, loss of or grey hair, a shorter distance between the nose and chin (if false teeth have been removed), glasses, liver spots on the hands, bowed legs and stooped backs. And, of course, there are the appropriate appendages and related signifiers, such as "walking canes," "walkers" or "wheel chairs." (Powell and Longino 2002)

At the other extreme, there are positive representations of aging via, for example, fictional characters from the J. R. Tolkien's *Lord of the Rings* that epitomize an agelessness, immortality, and wisdom in the role of wizardry. Nevertheless, the issue of gender and the body is crucial to understand the full complexity of aging in contemporary society.

Theorizing Embodiment, Postmodernism and Aging 39

THE GENDERED AGING BODY

Although we have analyzed modernist theoretical movements of functionalism, political economy of old age, and feminist gerontology, they ignore a postmodern understanding of aging identity, the body, cultural representations of aging, and gendered images of aging. The "gendered body" itself is a discursive site in which power is produced, acted upon, engaged with, and received. These aspects of power allow spaces for resistance to emerge, enabling power to be positive and at the same time negative. The experiences and knowledge of life before, in the celebrated young body and in the life threads of familial responsibilities and motherhood or fatherhood, can enable or disable the individual for success on the aging platform.

Theoretical arguments on gender sometimes fall prey to the philosophical error of essentialism: the appeal to metanarratives that claim to capture universal processes underlying essential differences between men and women and are insensitive to local knowledge and diversity (Harper 1997). Rather, the body is like a hinge, a pivot point, between two realities. Grosz (1994) asserts that the body is neither, while being both. Some of these binary categories are inside/outside, subject/object, and active/passive. It is not that older women are one way and older men the opposite. Bodies, whether men or women, are both ways. It is primarily their relationship to power that makes them different.

Women's stories are often about their relationship to their bodies; men's are not. Women "use" their bodies as an asset to accomplish their goals more than men do. Therefore, according to Shilling (1993), they are more likely than men to develop their bodies as objects of perception for others. The downside of this conscious embodiment of women is that as they age, they tend to lose a key asset, and thus come to think of themselves, and to be thought of, as invisible. If beauty and sexual allure are perishable values, men's power is embedded in status and wealth, more enduring values that tend to increase, not diminish, with age. The impact of the diminished assets of female identity is undeniable. Angie Dickenson, a sixty-eight-year-old

American actress, reflecting on her experience of female embodiment and aging, put it well in an interview in a popular magazine:

> I'm surprised by every photograph I see of myself, because I don't look like I used to. I am not shocked anymore, just disappointed. I did look pretty good. I was all heart and sexiness, and that came from within. I had beautiful eyes, and unfortunately in trying to help them, I practically destroyed them with plastic surgery. I wish I looked now how I looked before, when I was young. (Life 2000, quoted in Longino and Powell 2004, 112)

Oberg and Tornstam (1999) found no evidence for the notion that women become more discontented with their bodies as they grow older, as compared with men. When asked to agree or disagree with the statement "I am satisfied with my body," about 80 percent of men agreed, regardless of their age. Only about two-thirds of young women agreed. But women in a successively older decade tended to agree more with the statement until there was essentially no difference between men and women after age sixty-five. It is younger women, not the older ones, who are the most dissatisfied.

The "body" within modernist theories of social gerontology pays insufficient attention to the ways in which gendered bodies have always enjoyed varying degrees of absence or presence in old age: in the guise of "female corporeality" and "male embodiment" (Gittens 1997). Indeed, there are discursive strategies whereby "the body" and "the social" are dissociated in the first place. In this framework, woman is saturated with, while man is divested of, corporeality. Older women have higher rates of chronic illnesses than do men, and their bodies outlast those of men. In clinical settings old women outnumber old men in nearly all waiting rooms. Yet the woman is divested while the man is invested with "the social," implying that knowledge is "gendered" and is male. The absent women in social gerontology were the women in the body excluded from the social. It is male bodies that animate the social; they appear for a fleeting moment, only to disappear immediately, in the space between "corporeality" and "sociality." Thus, it is not simply a case of recuperating bodies into the social, but of excavating the gendered discourses whereby gendered bodies were

Theorizing Embodiment, Postmodernism and Aging

differently inscribed into and out of the social in the first place. The crucial point here is not the more familiar story of her saturation with corporeality but the less familiar one of what happened to his body. As a needed qualification, Harper (1997, 169), reminds us that because women are always embodied and men are not, "men become embodied as they age through the experience of the experiential and constructed body." So the gap between women and men may narrow, in some ways, as they age.

Indeed, feminist social theorists beyond macro-based "feminist gerontology" have underlined the limits of Cartesian thought, which considered the subject as disembodied and, above all, asexual (Braidotti 1994). In the representation of the female body, the dichotomy between body and mind has been used to emphasize sexual difference. On the one hand, we have masculinity, which is defined in relation to the mind and the logos, while the feminine is defined in relation to the body and its procreative functions: an essentialist construction, par excellence (Twigg 2000). As Adrienne Rich reminds us, women have had to deconstruct the patriarchal stereotype that links the female body with its procreative function: "I am really asking whether women cannot begin, at last, to think through the body, to connect what has been so cruelly disorganized" (1976, 184). With this incisive sentence, Rich stresses that women have to overcome the damning dichotomy between soul and body in order to reappropriate their bodies and to create a female subject, in which the two entities are complementary. Women often find themselves defined as "the other" (the residual category) against men, just as black people do against white people and gay people do against heterosexual people (Harper 1997). As Harper (1997) points out, they are the ones in the shadows, not in the positions of power; the defined, not the definers. For example, as we discussed earlier, contemporary cultural representations of aging focus on the body because this provides the clearest evidence of the historical inequality between gender differentiation that the body of women is inscribed with oppressive ideological mystifications (Friedan 1993; Sontag 1991). Western literature and iconography are full of anthropomorphic discursive representations of old age as a woman with "grey hair," "withered," "faded," "pale and wan face," "foul and obscene" (Friedan 1993).

From this discussion, it would seem that the aging body is yet another mode of embodied subjectivity for gerontologists to unravel. The re-territorialization of the aging body by society, and paradigmatically by social gerontology, is a strategy that parallels the denial of wider social theory within the main traditions of social gerontology (Bengston, Burgess, and Parrot 1997). We have suggested that the concept of the "body" itself may take on particular sets of meanings for older people, both men and women, whose subjectivity of identity formation may conflict or legitimize cultural representations of aging.

The notion of "intertextuality" can be used as it is a mechanism by which the social world is fabricated, and this explains why cultural ideologies continually perpetuate perceptions of aging and gender. Postmodern perspectives can facilitate an understanding of how older people can intertextually reconstruct cultural narratives to explain their representations of identity and self-identity. Such a strategy involves a challenge to the homogeneity of the social category "elderly" as an embodiment of the "time's up" medical narrative. When the issue of social identity in later life is analyzed, Foucault's (1977) contention seems powerful in articulating that there has been a growth in the localities of power and knowledge that seek to inscribe physical and social bodies with discourses of normality and self-government. In the search for a stable identity not dominated by both professional and cultural discourses of power, older people must "achieve" it through "ontological reflexivity" (Giddens 1991). Accordingly, the self-identity needs to be consciously constructed and maintained. The aging self has a new existential pathway to follow, stepping outside dominant discourses of medical and patriarchal reason, to include a process of safety, self-exploration, self-struggle, and self-discovery (Powell and Longino 2002).

Contrary to Eurocentric philosophical traditions, feminist philosophical studies have emphasized that the body is a symbolic construct, located in a specific historical and cultural context: in other words its conceptualization can no longer ignore the close nexus between gender, class, and race (Blaikie 1999; Twigg 2000). Further, a significant issue for the articulation of aging with gender to further understand the "body" is represented by the theories

Theorizing Embodiment, Postmodernism and Aging 43

of Foucault (1977) and Sontag (1991), which show the extent to which institutional medicine objectifies the "sick" body, once it has been biomedicalized (Powell 2001f). Foucault (1977) claims that medical practices produce the "soul" of the individual by disciplining the body and corporealizing medical spaces. Indeed, the success of modernity's domination over efficient bodies in industry, docile bodies in prisons, patient bodies in clinical research, and regimented bodies in schools and residential centers attest to Foucault's thesis that the human body is a highly adaptable terminus for the circulation of power relations (Powell and Biggs 2001; Armstrong 1983).

We have illuminated some of the paradoxes implicit in society, characterized by the historical discourses of decline and how they are embedded in popular culture relating to aging body and gendered body. Nevertheless, the next section shows how biotechnology networks work to project a conformist and consumerist view of the body, testifying to a different perception of the aging body by machine modification, a movement away from "expert" discourse to a new language based on "consumer identity" and "subjectivity" (Haraway 1991; Gilleard and Higgs 2000).

The recent information revolution has forced us once again to question the relationship between the body and the machine. If it is true that the continuous bombardment of television images of mutilated and cut-up bodies has, so to speak, dematerialized them, on the other hand, the corporeality of the body comes obsessively back (Powell and Longino 2002; Longino and Powell 2004). However, computer communication has done away with bodily presence, and the new technologies make us see the machine as an extension of our bodies (Haraway 1991). The questions posed by this revolution in the dissemination of information are difficult to answer. It is no longer a question of emphasizing, in prophetic and apocalyptic tones, the end of humanism but rather of understanding how and to what extent technology and science can help us to change, since technology is ultimately inextricable from our aging body, becoming an apparatus which is at the same time material and symbolic. The cyborg, a fusion between machine and organic body, opens up an immense universe of possibility: nowadays, we no longer speak of organic bodies but of transorganic bodies, post-human bodies and bodies in the net (Haraway 1991; Longino and Powell 2004).

These diverse forms of bodily form hold out the promise of "utopian bodies," a movement away from static medical constrainment and objectification to much more self-subjectification practices (Morris 1998; Powell and Biggs 2004). Indeed, Haraway's (1991) original reference to cyborgic fusion of biological and machine entities has been enthusiastically taken up by postmodern gerontology. The list of biotechnologies available extends beyond traditional prosthesis to include virtual identities created by and reflected in the growing number of "silver surfers" using the Internet as a free-floating form of identity management. Thus Featherstone and Wernick (1995, 3) claim that it is now possible to reconstruct "the body itself" as biomedical and information technologies make available "the capacity to alter not just the meaning, but the very material infrastructure of the body. Bodies can be re-shaped, remade, fused with machines, empowered through technological devices and extensions."

The increasing popularization of such key terms for reinvented bodies as "machine bodies" implies an effect of producing an intrasubjective consciousness and a conspicuousness of behavior, either for bodily change or against it. Moral action, whether it is individual or collective, involves the self knowing the self, a process of self-formation as an ethical aging subject (Powell and Biggs 2004). Self-responsibility, when passed through the notion of the "sick body," becomes a covert form of moral judgment upon which decisions to supply or deny often expensive forms of biotechnology can be made (Powell and Biggs 2004). Indeed, one is unwell because one is unhealthy, and one is unhealthy because the proper steps of self-care had not been taken in the past. So why should others have to provide scarce resources to make good this moral turpitude? Such an attitude to the healthy body presents moral decisions on the supply and demand for services in the "neutral" language of technomedical science (Powell and Biggs 2004). However, the outcome is that the prudent do not need it, while the imprudent do not deserve it. Any allusion here to economic planning and to pension policy is more than passing, for in both cases it is the resource-rich who can afford, but may rarely need, such technology, whereas the resource-poor

Theorizing Embodiment, Postmodernism and Aging 45

cannot afford it (Moody 1998; Phillipson 1998). For example, biotechnology can sell as "truth" a dream of "not growing old" to older people (Powell and Biggs 2004). However, it is the self-experience of aging subjects that can refute, deny, and accept the "truth" claims of biotechnology (Rose 1996). In the case of lifestyles of the aging, the active adoption of particular consumer practices such as uses of biotechnology contributes to a narrative that is both compensatory and "ageless" in its construction of self (Biggs and Powell 2001). The aging body culturally represents the best hiding place for internal illnesses that remained inconspicuous until the advent of biotechnologies (Frank 1996). Subjective relations to the self will be affected to the extent that biotechnologies confront older people with the proposition that this subjective truth: the truth of their relation to themselves and to others may be revealed by their "aging bodies." If this is legitimate, we may anticipate through "biology and culture" (Morris 1998) the problematic of illnesses associated with aging rejoining the sphere of bioethics through the back door. "Illness" and "body repair" as problematized by biotechnology will again belong to the strategic margin that older people embody as subjects of purposeful action.

There are obvious tensions between the biotechnological commodification of old age. It is through constructing and transgressing the aging body, by subverting the "stigma" surrounding later life (Powell and Biggs 2000), and thus redefining physical capital (May 1996) that many old bodies resisted the fixed images of old age. Moreover, within this discursive space of biotechnology the construction of the aging body allows elders to become their own significant other, to challenge the gaze of others and to "be for themselves." Their reconstructed bodies, therefore, become sites of empowerment whether they collude or resist ageist stereotypes.

CONCLUSION

This chapter has drawn insights from postmodernism, which provides compelling questions of how we interpret, problematize, and understand the body as dancing in-between subject/object. Hence, the chapter has demonstrated how the body is not separate from the body subject (May 1996) but is intertwined. Arthur Frank (1991, 1996) argues that, simultaneously, the embodied agent becomes a producer of society while at the same time it is society that creates the embodied agent.

It is by reimagining the boundaries of the body that we can begin to understand how the gaze inscribes itself unintelligibly on the aging body. The argument that has been presented here demonstrates an understanding of the body as both lived through and as constructed. The study of the body in gerontological literature needs to engage with the real materiality of bodies and at the same time understand the ways in which bodies are performed, represented, and positioned.

Central to this discussion is how the inscription of aging, popular culture, gender, and biotechnology are placed on and work in tandem with the rhythms of the body. The body is constantly operating within fields of temporality, in which mobile networks of relations produce and transmit power/knowledge to the object vis-à-vis subject (Butler 2000). Thus the body operates within fields of power and within the realm of signs. It has been argued that time and identity in society consist of a multiplicity of discursive elements that come into play at various times, thus existing in "different and even contradictory discourses" (Foucault 1982, 100–102). The body is a "visage," a collection of signs to be interpreted. It becomes a façade (cf. Biggs 1993), which at the same time both conceals and expresses the inner being. It is by centralizing the historical development of the body in social theory that one can illustrate and interrogate how the architecture of the ageist discourse recodes their now "profaned" bodies. Constructing some bodies as marginal and excluding them from mainstream representations defines boundaries and gives legitimacy to society's claims of what is a "natural" way for a body to look.

The body is a dynamic, nebulous form and always in the process of becoming. The contours of the body outline a visible but transitional object (Featherstone and Wernick 1995). But, as Powell and Longino (2001) argue, there is no surety of what the body is. What one can argue from discussion of the body is that it becomes the threshold through which the subject's lived experience of the world is incorporated and interpolated and, as such, can

Theorizing Embodiment, Postmodernism and Aging   47

never be purely understood. The aging body is a "transitional entity"; power is produced, generated, and negotiated in terms of the inscriptions placed on the aging body in micro and local domains.

Indeed, by taking a localized approach, postmodern gerontology has been more adaptable than any "grand narrative" to address issues of power and oppression (Seidman 1994, 207). By focusing on the aging body and how culture impinges on its subject formation, postmodern gerontology goes beyond fixed classifications of modern ideas deriving from biomedical sciences as well as grand narratives of macrotheories of aging (Longino and Powell 2004; Powell 2001c). This is a view consolidated by Bauman (2001), who points to the way that society has become increasingly individualized. All individual lives are affected by localized conditions and narratives, and what is needed is an analysis of the extent to which the individual is governed by external conditions in terms of their life choices (Bauman 2001, 6–7). Bauman argued that postmodern culture is effectively a competitive market, trading in "life meanings" (Bauman 2001, 4), and this can be linked to Lyotard's suggestion that knowledge has become the product of different "specialisms" to be bought and sold for profit (Lyotard 1984, 5). For example, the fragmentation of the aging body has become a commodifiable social space through which biotechnologies can offer body reconstruction in consumer-led Western society through machine extensions to the body (Powell and Longino 2002).

Similarly, Frederic Jameson (1991) understood postmodernism as an extension of the "logic of late capitalism." Jameson argued that globalization and multinational capitalism had resulted in mass consumerism and the total commodification of culture, in which "images, styles and representations are the products themselves" (Connor 1989, 46). However, Stuart Hall argues that the postmodern idea of cultural homogenization is too simplistic (Hall 1992, 304). He suggests that in a restructuring of social theory we should acknowledge how the global and the local articulate and recognize that globalization is unevenly distributed and is also a Western phenomenon indicative of the unequal power relations between the west and the rest. Estes, Biggs, and Phillipson (2003) consolidate this by suggesting that

Occidental globalization affects the poverty status of older people universally.

Nevertheless, the great strength of postmodernism is to dissect fixed discourses of modernity and reveal alternative cultural processes that impinge on both epistemic and ontologically flexible narratives pertaining to the human body. As Seidman states, modernist social theory was focused on neat divisions, hierarchies, and foundational premises, and the aim of sociologists was to find universalisms (Seidman 1994, 347). Postmodernism, on the other hand, was to look at subject formation regarding the body as it has been overlooked by macromodernist theories. The next chapter assesses the importance of a narrative gerontology to have a deeper understanding of aging identity.

Chapter 3

TOWARDS A NARRATIVE GERONTOLOGY

The previous chapter explored postmodernism and aging identity in social gerontology. There has been much research in recent times that has called for a 'reflexive gerontology' (Powell 2010). Research on aging as a postmodern conceptual tool is important. To add to the reflexive project, is to incorporate concepts and methodologies applicable to understanding aging identity: narrative. "Narrativity" has become established in the social sciences, both as a method of undertaking and interpreting research (cf Kenyon et al. 1999; Holstein and Gubrium 2000; Biggs et al. 2003) and as a technique for modifying the self (McAdams 1993; Mcleod 1997). Both Gubrium (1992) and Katz (1999) suggest that older people construct their own analytical models of personal identity based on lived experience and on narratives already existing in their everyday environments. By using a narrative approach, the meaning of family can be told through stories about the self as well as ones "at large" in public discourse.

"Discourse" is a notion more often used to denote a relatively fixed set of stories that individuals or groups have to conform to in order to take up a recognized and legitimate role. Such an understanding of discourse can be found in the earlier work of Michel Foucault (1977) and others (Powell and Biggs 2001). Self-storying, draws attention to the ways in which family identities are both more open to negotiation and are more likely to be "taken in" in the sense of being owned and worked on by individuals themselves.

At the same time, there has been an increasing interest in aging and family, within sociological developments relating to aging and social policy since the late 1990s (Minkler 1998). This is a trend that has cut across Canadian, American, and European research (Cloke et al 2006; Walker and Naegele 1999; Minkler 1998; Bengtson et al. 2000; Biggs and Powell 2001; Carmel et al. 2007). The reasons for such expansion are as much economic and political as they are academic. US and European governments recognize that the "family" is important for social and economic needs and this should be reflected in our understanding of aging, family processes, and in social policy (Beck, 2005). This leads to the question: How can we theoretically contextualize this and what are lessons for family research in sociological theorizing?

Families, of course, are made up of interpersonal relationships within and between generations that are subject to both the formal rhetoric of public discourses, and the self-stories that bind them together in everyday life. The notion of family is, then, an amalgam of policy discourse and everyday negotiation and as such alerts us to the wider social implications of those relationships (cf Powell 2005).

The rhetoric of social policy and the formal representations of adult aging and family life that one finds there, provide a source of raw material for the construction of identity and a series of spaces in which such identities can be legitimately performed. It is perhaps not overstating the case to say that the "success" of a family policy can be judged from the degree to which people live within the stories or narratives of family created by it.

In fact, the relationship between families and older people has been consecutively re-written in the social policy literature. Each time a different story has been told and different aspects of the relationship have been thrown into high relief. It might even be argued that the family has become a key site upon which expected norms of intergenerational relations and late-life citizenship are being built. This chapter explores the significance of such narratives, using developments in the United Kingdom as a case example that may also shed light on wider contemporary issues associated with old age.

The structure of the chapter is fourfold. Firstly, we start by mapping out the emergence and consolidation of neoliberal family policy and its relationship to emphasis on family obligation, state surveillance, and active citizenship. Secondly, we highlight both the ideological continuities and discontinuities of the subsequent social democratic turn and their effects on older people and the family. Thirdly, research studies are drawn on to highlight how "grand-parenting" has been recognized by governments in recent years, as a particular way of "storying" the relationship between old age and family life. Finally, we explore ramifications for researching family policy and old age by pointing out that narratives of inclusion and exclusion often coexist. It is suggested that in the future, aging and family life will include the need to negotiate multiple policy narratives. At an interpersonal level, sophisticated narrative strategies would be required if a sense of familial continuity and solidarity is to be maintained.

NEOLIBERALISM, AGING, AND THE FAMILY

Political and social debate since the Reagan/Thatcher years, has been dominated by neoliberalism, which postulates the existence of autonomous, assertive, rational individuals who must be protected and liberated from "big government" and state interference (Gray 1995). Indeed, Walker and Naegele (1999) claim a startling continuity across Europe is the way "the family" has been positioned by governments as these ideas have spread beyond their original "English speaking" base.

Neoliberal policies on the family has almost always started from a position of laissez-faire, except when extreme behavior threatens its members or wider social relations (Beck, 2005). It can be seen that that neoliberal policy came to focus on two main issues. And, whilst both only represent the point at which a minimalist approach from the state touches family life, they come to mark the dominant narrative through which aging and family are made visible in the public domain (Cloke et al. 2006).

On the one hand, increasing attention was paid to the role families took in the care of older people who were either mentally or physically infirm. A series of policy initiatives (UKG, 1981, 1989, 1990) recognized that families were a principal source of care and support. "Informal" family care became a key building block of policy toward an aging population. It both increased the salience of traditional family values, and independence from government and enabled a reduction in direct support form the state.

On the other hand, helping professionals, following US experience (Pillemer and Wolf 1986), became increasingly aware of the abuse that older people might suffer and the need to protect vulnerable adults from a variety of forms of abuse and neglect (Biggs et al. 1995). Policy guidance, "*No Longer Afraid: The Safeguard of Older People in Domestic Settings,*" was issued in 1993, shortly after the move to seeing informal care as the mainstay of the welfare of older people. As the title suggests, this was also directed primarily at the family.

It is perhaps a paradox that a policy based ostensibly on the premises of leaving-be combines two narrative streams that result in increased surveillance of the family. This paradox is based largely on these points being the only ones where policy "saw" aging in families, rather than ignoring it. This is not to say that real issues of abuse and neglect fail to exist, even though British politicians have often responded to them as if they were some form of natural disaster unrelated to the wider policy environment. To understand the linking of these narratives, it is important to examine trends tacit in the debate on family and aging, but central to wider public policy.

Wider economic priorities, to "roll back the state" and thereby release re-sources for individualism and free enterprise, had become translated into a family discourse about caring obligations and the need to enforce them. If families ceased to care, then the state would have to pick up the bill. It was not that families were spoken of as being naturally abusive. Neither was the "discovery" of familial abuse linked to community care policy outside academic debate (Biggs 1996). Discourses on the rise of abuse and on informal care remained separate in the formal policy domain. However, a subtle change of narrative tone had taken place. Families, rather than being

Towards a Narrative Gerontology

seen as "havens against a harsh world," were now easily perceived as potential sites of mistreatment, and the previously idealized role of the unpaid carer became that of a potential recalcitrant, attempting to avoid their family obligations. An attempt to protect a minority of abused elders thus took the shape of a tacit threat, hanging above the head of every aging family (Biggs and Powell 2000). It is worth note that these policy developments took little account of research evidence indicating that family solidarity and a willingness to care had decreased in neither the United Kingdom (Wenger 1994; Phillipson 1998) nor the United States (Bengtson and Achenbaum 1993). Further, it appeared that familial caring was actually moving away from relationships based on obligation and toward ones based on negotiation (Finch and Mason, 1993).

Family commitment has, for example, varied depending upon the characteristic care-giving patterns within particular family units. Individualistic families provided less instrumental help and made use of welfare services, whereas a second, collectivist pattern offered greater personal support. Whilst this study focused primarily on upward generational support, Silverstein and Bengtson (1997) observed that "tight-knit" and "detached" family styles were often common across generations. Unfortunately, policy developments have rarely taken differences in care-giving styles into account, preferring a general narrative of often idealized role relationships. It is not unfair to say that during the neoliberal period, the dominant narrative of family became that of a site of care going wrong.

SOCIAL DEMOCRACY, AGING, AND THE FAMILY

Social democratic policies toward the family arose from the premise that by the early 1990s, the free-market policies of the /Reagan/Thatcher years had seriously damaged the social fabric of the nation state and that its citizens needed to be encouraged to identify again with the national project. A turn to an alternative, sometimes called "the third way," emerging under Clinton, Blair and Schroeder administrations in the United States and parts of Europe, attempted to find means of mending that social fabric, and as part of it, relations between older people and their families (Beck, 2005). The direction that the new policy narrative took is summarized in UK Prime Minister Blair's (1996) statement that "the most meaningful stake anyone can have in society is the ability to earn a living and support a family." Work, or failing that, work-like activities, plus an active contribution to family life began slowly to emerge, delineating new narratives within which to grow old (Hardill et al. 2007).

Giddens (1998) in the United Kingdom and Beck (1998) in Germany, both proponents of social democratic politics, have claimed that citizens are faced with the task of piloting themselves and their families through a changing world in which globalization has transformed our relations with each other, now based on avoiding risk. According to Giddens (1998), a new partnership is needed between government and civil society. Government support to the renewal of community through local initiative, would gives an increasing role to voluntary organizations, encourages social entrepreneurship and significantly, supports the democratic family characterized by equality, mutual respect, autonomy, decision-making through communication and freedom of violence. It is argued that social policy should be less concerned with equality and more with inclusion, with community participation reducing the moral and financial hazard of dependence (cf Walker 2002; Biggs et al. 2003; Powell and Owen 2007; Walker and Aspalter 2008).

Through an increased awareness of the notion of ageism, the influence of European ideas about social inclusion and North American social communitarianism, families and older people found themselves transformed into active citizens who should be encouraged to participate in society, rather than be seen as a potential burden upon it (Biggs, 2001). A contemporary UK policy document, entitled *"Building a Better Britain for Older People"* (Department of Social Security 1998) is typical of a new genre of Western policy, re-storying the role of older adults. It suggests that the contribution of older people is vital, both to families and to voluntary organisations and charities. We believe their roles as mentors, providing ongoing support and advice to families, young people and other older people, should be recognised. Older people already show a considerable commitment to volunteering. The Government is working with voluntary groups and those representing older people to see how we can increase the quality and quantity of opportunities for older people who want to volunteer.

What is perhaps striking is that it is one of the few places where families are mentioned in an overview on older people, with the exception of a single mention of carers, many of whom, it is pointed out, "are pensioners themselves." In both cases the identified role for older people constitutes a reversal of the narrative offered in preceding policy initiatives. The older person like other members of family structure is portrayed as an active member of the social milieu, offering care and support to others (Hardill et al. 2007).

The dominant preoccupation of this policy initiative, is not however, concerned with families. Rather, there is a change of emphasis toward the notion of aging as an issue of lifestyle, and as such draws on contemporary gerontological observations of the "blurring" of age-based identities (Featherstone and Hepworth, 1995) and the growth of the grey consumer (Katz, 1999).

Whilst such a narrative is attractive to pressure groups, voluntary agencies and, indeed, social gerontologists; there is, just as with the policies of the neoliberals, an underlying economic motive which may or may not be to the long term advantage to older people and their families. Again, as policies develop, the force driving the story of elders as active citizens was to be found in policies of a fiscal nature. The most likely place to discover how the new story of aging, fits the bigger picture is in government-wide policy. In this case the document has been entitled "Winning the Generation Game" (UKG, 2000a). This begins well with "One of the most important tasks for twenty-first century Britain is to unlock the talents and potential of all its citizens. Everyone has a valuable contribution to make, throughout their lives." However, the reasoning behind this statement becomes clearer when policy is explained in terms of a changing demographic profile: "With present employment rates" it is argued, "one million more over-50s would not be working by 2020 because of growth in the older population. There will be 2 million fewer working-age people under 50 and 2 million more over 50: a shift equivalent to nearly 10 percent of the total working population."

The solution, then, is to engage older people not only part of family life but also in work, volunteering, or mentoring. Older workers become a reserve labor pool, filling the spaces left by falling numbers of younger workers. They thus contribute to the economy as producers as well as consumers and make fewer demands on pensions and other forms of support. Those older people who are not thereby socially included can engage in the work-like activity of volunteering.

Most of these policy narratives only indirectly affect the aging family. Families only have a peripheral part to play in the story and do not appear to be central to the lives of older people. However, it is possible to detect the same logic at work when attention shifts from the public to the private sphere. Here the narrative stream develops the notion of "grand-parenting" as a means of social inclusion. This trend can be found in the United Kingdom, in France (Girard and Ogg, 1998), Germany (Scharf and Wenger, 1995), as well as in the United States (Minkler, 1999).

In the British context the most detailed reference to grand-parenting can be found in an otherwise rather peculiar place, namely from the Home Office, which is an arm of British Government primarily concerned with law and order. In a document entitled "*Supporting Families*" (2000b), "family life" we are told, "is the foundation on which our communities, our society and our country are built." "Business people, people from the community, students and grandparents" are encouraged to join a schools mentoring network. Further, "the interests of grandparents, and the contribution they make, can be marginalized by service providers who, quite naturally, concentrate on dealing with parents. We want to change all this and encourage grandparents and other relatives to play a positive role in their families." By which it is meant: "home, school links or as a source of social and cultural history" and support when "nuclear families are under stress." Even older people who are not themselves grandparents can join projects "in which volunteers act as "grandparents" to contribute their experience to a local family."

Towards a Narrative Gerontology 57

In the narratives of social democracy, the aging family is seen as a reservoir of potential social inclusion. Older people are portrayed as holding a key role in the stability of both the public sphere, through work and volunteering, and in the private sphere, primarily through grandparental support and advice (Cloke et al. 2006). Grandparents, in particular, are storied as mentors and counselors across the public and private spheres.

Whilst the grandparental title has been used as a catch-all within the dominant policy narrative; bringing with it associations of security, stability and an in many ways an easier form of relationship than direct parenting it exists as much in public as in private space. It is impossible to interpret this construction of grandparenthood without placing it in the broader project of social inclusion, itself a response to increased social fragmentation and economic competition. Indeed it may not be an exaggeration to refer this construal of grand-parenting as neofamilial. In other words, the grandparent has out-grown the family as part of a policy search to include older adults in wider society. The grandparent becomes a mentor to both parental and grandparental generations as advice is not restricted to schools and support in times of stress, but also through participation in the planning of amenities and public services (BGOP 2000).

This is a very different narrative of older people and their relationship to families, from that of the dependent and burdensome elder. In the land of policy conjuring, previously conceived problems of growing economic expense and social uselessness have been miraculously reversed. Older people are now positioned as the solution to problems of demographic change, rather than their cause. They are a source of guidance to ailing families, rather than their victims. Both narratives increase the social inclusion of a potentially marginal social group: Formerly known as the elderly.

"GRAND-PARENTING" POLICY

There is much to be welcomed in this story of the active citizen elder especially so if policy-inspired discourse and lived self-narratives are taken to be one and the same. There are also certain problems, however, if the two are unzipped, particularly when the former is viewed through the lens of what we know about families from other sources.

First, each of the roles identified in the policy domain, volunteering, mentor-ship and grand-parenting, have a rather second–hand quality. By this is meant that each is supportive to another player who is central to the task at hand. Rather like within Erikson's psycho-social model of the lifecycle, the role allocated to older people approximates grand-generativity and thereby contingent upon the earlier, but core life task of generativity itself (Kivnick 1988). In other words it is contingent upon an earlier part of life and the narratives woven around it, and fails to distinguish an authentic element of the experience of aging.

When the roles are examined in this light, a tacit secondary status begins to emerge. Volunteering becomes unpaid work: Mentoring, support to helping professionals in their eroded pastoral capacities; and grand-parenting, in its familial guise, a sort of peripheral parent without the hassle. This peripherality may be in many ways desirable, so long as there is an alternative pole of authentic attraction that ties the older adult into the social milieux. Either that or the narrative should allow space for legitimized withdrawal from socially inclusive activities. Unfortunately the dominant policy narrative has little to say on either count.

Second, there is a shift of attention away from the most frail and oldest old, to a third age of active or positive aging, which, incidentally, may or may not take place in families. It is striking that a majority of policy documents of what might be called the "new aging" start counting from age fifty, an observation that is true for formal government rhetoric and pressure from agencies and initiatives lead by elders (Biggs, 2001). This interpretation of the life-course has been justified in terms of its potential for forming intergenerational alliances (BGOP, 2000) and fits well with the economic priority of drawing on older people as a reserve labor force (UKG 2000b).

Third, there is a striking absence of analysis of family relations at that age. Possibilities of intergenerational conflict as described in other literature (De Beauvoir, 1979), not least in research into three-generation family

Towards a Narrative Gerontology 59

therapy (Hargrave and Anderson, 1992; Qualls, 1999), plus the everyday need for tact in negotiating childcare roles (Bornat et al. 1999; Waldrop et al. 1999), appear not to have been taken into account. This period in the aging life-course is often marked by midlife tension and multi-generational transitions, such as those experienced by late adolescent children and by an increasingly frail top generation (Ryff and Seltzer, 1996). Research has indicated that solidarity between family generations is not uniform, and will involve a variety of types and degrees of intimacy and reciprocity (Silverstein and Bengtson 1997).

Finally, little consideration has been given to the potential conflict between the tacit hedonism of aging lifestyles based on consumption and those more socially inclusive roles of productive contribution, of which the "new grand-parenting" has become an important part. Whilst there are few figures on grandparental activity it does, for example, appear that community volunteering amongst older people is embraced with much less enthusiasm than policy-makers would wish (Boaz et al. 1999). Chambre (1993) claims volunteering in the US diminishes in old age. Her findings indicate the highest rates of volunteering occur in mid-life, where nearly two thirds volunteer. This rate declines to 47 percent for persons aged between 65 and 74 and to 32 percent among persons 75 and over. A United Kingdom Guardian-ICM (2000) poll of older adults indicated that, amongst grandfathers, but not grandmothers, there was a degree of suspicion of child-care to support their own children's family arrangements. More than a quarter of men expressed this concern, compared with only 19 percent of women interviewed. The United Kingdom charity, Age Concern, stated: "One in ten grandparents are under the age of 56. They have 10 more years of work and are still leading full lives."

One might speculate, immersed in this narrative stream, that problematic family roles and relationships cease to exist for the work-returning, volunteering and community enhancing 50-plus "elder." Indeed, the major protagonists of social democracy seem blissfully unaware of several decades of research, particularly feminist research, demonstrating the mythical status of the "happy family" (cf e.g., Land, 1999).

What emerges from research literature on grand-parenting as it is included in people's everyday experience and narratives of self indicates two trends: (1) there appears to be a general acceptance of the positive value of relatively loose and undemanding exchange between first and third generations and (2) that deep commitments become active largely in situations of extreme family stress or breakdown of the middle generation.

First, grandparents have potential to influence and develop children through the transmission of values. Subsequently, grandparents serve as arbiters of knowledge and transmit knowledge that is unique to their identity, life experience, and history. In addition, grandparents can become mentors, performing the function of a generic life guide for younger children. This "transmission" role is confirmed by Mills' (1999) study of mixed gender relations and by Waldrop et al.'s (1999) report on grandfathering. According to Roberto (1990) early research on grand-parenting in the United States of America has attempted to identify the roles played by grandparents within the family system and towards grandchildren. Indeed, much US work on grand-parenting has focused on how older adults view and structure their relationships with younger people.

African American grandparents, for example, take a more active role, correcting the behavior of grandchildren and acting like "protectors" of the family. Accordingly, such behaviors are related to effects of divorce and under/unemployment. Research by Kennedy (1990) indicates, however, that there is a cultural void when it comes to grand-parenting roles for many white families with few guide-lines on how they should act as grandparents.

Girard and Ogg (1998) report that grand-parenting is a rising political issue in French family policy. They note that most grandmothers welcome the new role they have in child care of their grandchildren, but there is a threshold beyond which support interferes with their other commitments. Contact between older parents and their grandchildren is less frequent that with youngsters, with financial support becoming more prominent.

Two reports, explicitly commissioned to inform United Kingdom policy (Hayden et al. 1999; Boaz et al. 1999) classify grand-parenting under the general rubric of intergenerational relationships. Research evidence is cited, that "when thinking about the future, older people looked forward to their

Towards a Narrative Gerontology

role as grandparents" and that grandparents looked after their grandchildren and provided them with "love, support and a listening ear," providing childcare support to their busy children and were enthusiastic about these roles.

Hayden et al. (1999) used focus groups and qualitative interviewing and report that: "grand-parenting included spending time with grandchildren both in active and sedentary hobbies and pursuits, with many participants commenting on the mental and physical stimulation they gained from sharing activities with the younger generation. Coupled with this, the Beth Johnson Foundation (1998) found that older people as mentors had increased levels of participation with more friends and engendered more social activity. With the exception of the last study, each has relied on exclusive self-report data, or views on what grand-parenting might be like at some future point.

In research from the tradition of examining social networks, and thus not overtly concerned with the centrality of grand-parenting or grandparent-like roles as such, it is rarely identified as a key relationship and could not be called a strong theme. Studies on the United Kingdom, (Phillipson et al. 2000), Japan (Izuhara, 2000), the US (Schreck, 2000; Minkler, 1999), Hispanic Americans (Freidenberg, 2000), and Germany, (Chamberlayne and King, 2000) provide little evidence that grand-children, as distinct from adult children, are prominent members of older peoples reported social networks.

Grandparental responsibility becomes more visible if the middle generation is for some reason absent. Thompson, (1999) reports from the United Kingdom, that when parents part or die, it is often grandparents who take up supporting, caring and mediating roles on behalf of their grandchildren. The degree of involvement was contingent however on the quality of emotional closeness and communication within the family group. Minkler, (1999) has indicated that in the United States, one in ten grandparents has primary responsibility for raising a grandchild at some point, with care often lasting for several years.

This trend varies between ethnic groups, with 4.1 percent White, 6.55 percent Hispanic and 13.55 African American children living with their grandparents or other relatives. It is argued that a 44 percent increase in such responsibilities is connected to the devastating effects of wider social issues, including AIDS/HIV, drug abuse, parental homelessness and prison policy. Thomson and Minkler (2001) note that there is an increasing divergency in the meaning of grand-parenting between different socio-economic groups, with extensive care-givers (7 percent of the sampled population) having increasingly fewer characteristics in common with the 14.9 percent who did not provide child-care. In the United Kingdom, a similar split has been identified with 1 percent of British grandparents becoming extensive caregivers against a background pattern of occasional or minimal direct care (Duckworth, 2001).

It would appear that grand-parenting is not then, a uniform phenomenon, and extensive grand-parenting or grandparent-like activities are rarely an integral part of social inclusion. Rather, whilst it is seen as providing some intergenerational benefit, it may be a phenomenon that requires an element of un-intrusiveness and negotiation in its non-extensive form. When extensively relied on it is more likely to be a response to severely eroded inclusive environments and the self-protective reactions of families living with them. Minkler's analysis draws attention to race as a feature of social exclusion that is poorly handled by policy narratives afforded to the family and old age. There is a failure to recognize structural forms of inequality, and action seeking to socially include older people as a category appears to draw heavily on the occasional helper and social volunteer as a dominant narrative.

TOWARDS DIVERSE NARRATIVE STREAMS?

Each phase of social policy, be it the Reagan/Thatcher neoliberalism of the 1980s and early 1990s, the Clinton/Blairite interpretation of social democracy in the late 90s, or the millennial Bush or current Obama administration and David Cameron administration in the UK, leaves a legacy. Moreover, policy development is uneven and subject to local emphasis and elision, which means that it is quite possible for different, even conflicting narratives of family and later life to coexist in different parts of the policy system. Each period generates a discourse that can legitimate the lives of older people and family relations in particular ways and as their influence accrues, create the potential of entering into multiple narrative streams.

A striking feature of recent policy history has been that not only have the formal policies been quite different in their tenor and tacit objectives, one from another, they have also addressed different areas of the lives of aging families. Where there is little narrative overlap there is the possibility of both policies existing, however opposed they may be ideologically or in terms of practical outcome. Different narratives may colonize different parts of policy, drawing on bureaucratic inertia, political inattention, and convenience to maintain their influence. They have a living presence, not least when they impinge on personal aging.

Also, both policy discourses share a deep coherence, which may help to explain their co-existence. Each offers a partial view of aging and family life whilst downloading risk and responsibility onto aging families and aging identities. Neither recognizes aging which is not secondary to an independent policy objective. Both mask the possibility of authentic tasks of aging.

If the analysis outlined above is accepted, then it is possible to see contemporary social policy addressing diverse aspects of the family life of older people in differing and contradictory ways. Contradictory narratives for the aging family exist in a landscape that is both increasingly blurred in terms of roles and relationships and split-off in terms of narrative coherence and consequences for identity. Indeed in a future of complex and multiple policy agendas, it would appear that a narrative of social inclusion through active aging can coexist with one emphasizing carer obligation and surveillance. Such a co-existence may occasionally become inconvenient at the level of public rhetoric. However, at an experiential and ontological level, that is to say at the level of the daily lives of older adults and their families, the implications may become particularly acute. Multiple co-existing policy narratives may become a significant source of risk to identity maintenance within the aging family.

One has to imagine a situation in which later lives are lived, skating on a surface of legitimizing discourse. For everyday intents and purposes this surface supplies the ground on which one can build an aging identity and relate to other family members and immediate community. However, there is always the possibility of slipping, of being subject to trauma or transition. Serious slippage will provoke being thrown onto a terrain that had previously been hidden, an alternative narrative of aging with entirely different premises, relationship expectations and possibilities for personal expression. Policy narratives, however, are also continually breaking down and fail to achieve hegemony as they encounter lived experience. Indeed, it could be argued that a continuous process of re-constitution takes place via the play of competing narratives. When we are addressing the issue of older people's identity in later life we can usefully note Foucault's (1977) contention that there has been a growth in attempts to control national populations through discourses of normality, but at the same time this has entailed increasing possibilities for self-government.

Chapter 4

CONCLUSION:
TOWARDS GLOBAL THEORIES OF AGING

According to the 12th Annual World Wealth Report (2008), the wealth of people around the world with more than US$1 million in assets grew faster in 2007 than the world's economy. The world's economy exhibited a 5% gain in 2007; compared with a growth rate of over 9% among those with at least US$1 million in assets. Furthermore, the average wealth of these high net worth individuals (HNWIs) climbed to over US$ 4 million, exclusive of their residence. Interestingly, the greatest growth among HNWIs occurred in Eastern Europe, Latin America and Asia led by Brazil, Russia, India and China. When the "mass affluent" population (those with less than US$ 1 million but with substantial assets nonetheless) is added to the picture, the result is that the richest 20 percent of the world's population controls more than 75% of its wealth. In the past few decades there has been some striking gains among a relatively small percentage of the world's population (approximately 10 million out of 6.7 billion people can be classified as HNWIs) who are tapped into robust gains and wealth generation strategies (Annual World Wealth Report, 2008). The ascendancy of those forces concentrating high net worth wealth and capital accumulation among a narrow upper-crust is also capable of producing abject poverty among other segments of the population (Arias & Logan, 2002:197; Jessop, 2002).

It is the richest 1 percent of wealthy outliers who are benefiting from speculation and the deregulation of commerce and free trade (Powell & Cook 2010).

Some estimates conservatively place the gap between the richest and poorest nations at an all time high of more than 50 to 1 (Clark, 2007). Even with the stalling of mature economies, the gulf between the most advantaged and the most disadvantaged in developed countries is no less dramatic; factor in the impact of gender, ethnicity or other social impediments and the complexity intensifies as formidable inequalities shape well-being (Powell & Cook, 2010). The disparities extend well beyond vital income differentials to quality of life issues, education, structured dependencies or social exclusions resulting from policy decisions (Townsend, 2007). Navarro (2007) and others add their voice to Peter Townsend's assertion by noting that escalating differentials can be attributed in no small part to interventionist strategies adopted and endorsed by national governments. Not surprisingly, as a consequence of the richest segments of the population having far greater assets and control over their lives, they feel they have more in common with their counterparts in other regions than they do with their less affluent opposite number in their own regions (Hoogvelt, 1997). Cross-cultural comparisons are extraordinarily valuable in helping lay out causal connections and for double-checking inferences. For example, the Organization for Economic Co-operation and Development (OECD) has a reliable cross-national comparative database of indicators of social policy expenditures in 30 member nations and their state sponsored social welfare provisions entitled Social Expenditures (SocX) in the period 1980-2003. It covers public expenditures for typical forms of welfare including old age, survivors, incapacity-related benefits, health, family, active labor market programs, unemployment, housing, and other social policy areas (education excepted). Shalev (2007) points out that if health and pension benefits are combined as a share of GDP countries like Sweden rank at the top by devoting some 14% of its GDP to health and pension protections. Data for the period 1980-2001, the latest available on the OCED web-site, suggests that Germany expends about 8% and the United States and Japan about 4%.

Conclusion 67

GLOBALIZATION AND REFORMULATION OF ECONOMIC POWER

The proliferation of abetting ideologies evolving out of burgeoning free-market economies along with an accompanying diffusion of instrumental rationality, standardization, commoditization, or secularism have become embedded in our thinking, challenging all other relational metrics of daily life. In the process, modes of interaction and standards of assessing relational status or personal worth are recast. In both developed and emerging economies the nature of work and the meaning of careers are also undergoing major reformulations. There is a global softening of labor markets linked to downsizing of local employment opportunities, redundancies, a spate of subcontracting arrangements, and an economic volatility abetted by technological innovations that chip away at employment security, wage or benefit packages bringing a degree of economic and existential uncertainty to greater numbers of people. Of course such changes are not distributed evenly across all forms of employment, further exacerbating inequalities (Estes, Biggs and Phillipson, 2003).

It should also be stressed that adversity does not appear to strike women and men equally − and it is certainly reasonable to say that disadvantage begets gendered disadvantage when downturns occur (Powell & Cook, 2010). Women are disproportionately among the most disadvantaged and with age even greater hardships accrue to them. Adding to the intricacies of these unparalleled changes is the velocity with which they are taking place and the fact that they are accompanied by a deepening division between those whose principal pursuits are in subsistence or service sector markets and their counterparts who are primarily involved in large-scale export, international sectors, or equity markets. Together these forces are bringing about a profound imbalance within and between populations as one group shares in the generation of wealth while the other becomes increasingly dependent and is being subordinated to decisions made in the other sector, by a cartel half a world away (Bauman, 1998).

This is not to say that states are mere followers of transnational interests but it is no longer the case that nation-state sovereignty can be taken-for-granted in the policy realm. Nor is it necessarily the case that state policies are as all-powerful as they once were in shaping daily life (Dallmayer, 2005; Fraser, 2005). As Estes, Biggs and Phillipson (2003) so cogently assert, the welfare state of the last century has been replaced by a competitive state of the 21st century, always mindful of its global positioning (see also, Hudson & Lowe, 2004). Foucault (1978) coined the phrase "non-sovereign power" when he was discussing issues of bodily control. By drawing a nice analogy Yapa (2002:15) proposes that a parallel concept may provide insights into the vagaries of post-industrial public-sector decision making. To make sense of domestic versus international priorities and their effect on daily life, scholars would do well to come to terms with the notion of "non-sovereign power" as it applies to social justice, autonomy, monetary policies and capital mobility, and other forms of extra-national pressures emending local policies. We would assert that to date there has been a real lag between transnational developments and the way analysts think of social policies. Appadurai (2001) attributes the stumbling blocks in conceptualization to "…the disjunctures between various vectors characterizing this world-in-motion that produce fundamental problems of livelihood, equity, suffering, justice, and governance" (Appadurai, 2001: 6). In his characterization, proximate social issues have causes that are hardly local and call for non-parochial perspectives if they are to be addressed.

As Giddens maintains, one of the most significant impacts of globalization is that it has brought an "intensification of worldwide social relations which link distant localities in such a way that local happenings are shaped by events occurring many miles away and vice versa" (Giddens, 1990:64). As a consequence, few governments are eager to make decisions separately from their reliance on global enterprise; it is as though they are in a situation of shared sovereignty, having to negotiate between domestic, international, corporatist, and transnational interests (Esping-Andersen, 1990; Hill, 2006; Kennett, 2001; Navarro, 2007). NGOs such as the World Bank and the International Monetary Fund have also become architectural partners in local policy deliberations by sanctioning preferred welfare

Conclusion

policies as a condition of their support of monetization (Deacon, Hulse & Stubbs, 1997; Dembele, 2007; Hart, 2002). Even so, nation-states nonetheless serve important administrative functions in a world dominated by transnational corporate interests and it is unlikely that governmental responsibilities are either going to be usurped or allowed to wither in light of their functionality (Hill, 2006; Navarro, 2007). It is not too far fetched to say that certain transnational interests see themselves as having universal jurisdiction, assertions of state autonomy notwithstanding.

With the spreading of these transformations has come a reshuffling of local priorities, with governmental emoluments directed or redirected to areas defined as having the greatest public importance and bringing the greatest returns. Of course the realities behind that assertion are deserving of close scrutiny as the policy process is unquestionably political and the state must mediate rival claims as it serves as the principal mechanism by which revenues are collected and resources distributed. Meanwhile, social entitlements, expenditures, and daily experience for people who may not fully grasp the raison d'être behind their situations reflect these same priorities. Hill (2006) suggests that social policy regimes are regularly structured to be consistent with other forms of social stratification within a country. To the extent there is a convergence in social welfare policies around the globe it might not be mere coincidence that social stratification and social class divisions are growing more pronounced in the face of globalization. In light of global economic flows, the salience and permeability of national borders, whether in Europe, the western hemisphere, or in the East are a different matter than they were even half a century ago (Kearney, 1995).

In terms of both economics and domestic social policies, the impact of international economic relations has recontoured the landscape, so to speak, all the way to the regionalization and appropriation of economic relations. What were once bold lines of demarcation are now dotted lines more suggestive of administrative spheres than nationalistic borders. In the global century, deregulated markets are tightly integrated with political and social transformations, affecting local circumstances and communality (Geetz, 1973). All in all, the globalizing influences of the early 21st century are producing a distinctive era in social history linked to the emergence of transnational actors as well as economics and technologies that are helping fuel the shifts. Global economic change portends more than alterations in per capita income, the nature of financial products and currency markets, or the rapid circulation of goods, communication or technologies. It is precursor to broad cultural and political shifts that challenge pre-contact arrangements, notions of social justice and solidarity, as well as local interaction patterns. In a post-modern world, globalization is creating interlocking dependencies linked to the ways in which priorities are ordained by transnational interests. As Chen and Turner (2006) point out in a discussion focused on the welfare of the elderly but equally applicable to all social welfare, the accrual of public benefits reflects the invisible hand of market forces, the invisible handshake of tradition, and the invisible foot of political decisions. Despite avowals about the secularity of modern life, economic-thinking, what might be termed spreadsheet logic, is accorded near theological status, its canons seen as universally applicable and providing appropriate precept for adjudicating what is considered fair and just. These tendencies are abetted by what is sometimes called the cyber infrastructure, or more simply, informatics, reinforcing these shifts and creating a digital divide separating those on either edge of the diffusion of innovations. Of course there is more to this technological transformation than the appearance of new ways to communicate, it has also paved the way to a post-fordist formulation that Castells (2000) labels network capitalism.

GLOBALIZATION AND THE SOCIAL CONTRACT

We do not mean to imply that globalization comes as a unified package; it is nonetheless true that major changes have resulted from an ability to move capital around as summarily as desired to gain leverage, possibly destabilizing local financial and labor-markets in the process. Real questions have emerged about the autonomy of nation-states and the balancing of altruistic social expenditures with economic participation on the world stage. The tensions between social protections and global corporate connections

Conclusion   71

are contributing to what can aptly be called "social deficits" in which people are left to fend for themselves to the extent that they are able. In the face of inflation and related economic adversities, slashing social spending is routinely offered as a fitting resolution preferable to raising taxes for wealthy individuals or corporations (Mishra, 1999). The global span of information technologies and the advent of the global compass held by transnational corporations means they are able to shift extraction, manufacturing, fabrication and many service functions to whatever locale offers the most favorable economic returns, including tax structures. These and other consequences of globalization are fraught with new risks and ambiguities in daily experience and in the way matters of worth are defined; along with the many positive aspects that are undeniably part of the process associated with privatization.

In a synopsis of a few of the more evident effects of globalization, Navarro (2007) points to the privatization of services, public assets, and other public provisions in asymmetrical fashion; deregulation of labor and currency markets as well as other forms of commerce; free trade; escalation of an accompanying anti-interventionist rhetoric; encouragement of individualism and consumerism. A number of commentators have noted that a corollary of globalization results in an unprecedented pattern of social risk. As Townsend (2007) so elegantly points out, the globalization of the marketplace is changing the face of dependency. It is as though the configuration of risks has shifted from settling on just those poor, down and outers living along society's margins to those derailed by restructuring of labor markets, the dramatic spread of employment in service sector jobs, shifts in the types of career patterns that so characterized the 20th century, and the role of informatics affecting employability of middle-class workers.

These risks are not grounded merely in the absence of resources but in an absence of personal autonomy and by people's position relative to others. Add to these factors the fact that as they wrestle with the issues, national and local governments are assailed from multiple fronts; pressed by transnational interests to provide open trade liberalization for private enterprise; and pressed by the growing need for social protections and labor policies to sustain the working populace and those whose lives have fallen through the proverbial social safety net. Ever more inclusive protections call for targeted expenditures at exactly the time when expenditures are hemmed-in by capacity to levy taxes of any type but especially progressive taxes and by powerful interested constituencies. The neoliberal globalizing drive has disenfranchised workers and their representatives in ways that have eroded their ability to bargain for benefits. Many commentators have noted that governments have generally adopted a *laissez faire* stance when for one reason or another they have chosen not to intervene in the disempowerment of the citizenry (Navarro, 2007).

As a facet of a much broader movement toward privatization, governmental social services are adopting a market-based management model and relying on non-governmental agencies (NGOs) to take up the slack. There is a wide array of subtypes and expenditure patterns associated with every form but an underlying logic in nearly all instances is a push toward commodification or cost-effectiveness of the programs (couched in terms of return on investment measured by market-driven stipulations), in contrast to their ability to genuinely affect lives. Policy recipients not likely to provide economic returns on governmental investments in them tend to be defined as burdensome charity cases. There are extensive changes that may be adapted to local contextual factors reflecting long-standing norms, values, religions, policies, existing social metrics, and institutionalized arrangements even as they embody overtones imposed by international priorities (Dallmayer, 2005; Fraser, 2005). Unraveling the relative importance of domestic arrangements and transnational influences can be a tricky task, to say the least. It involves both an in-depth grasp of domestic issues and an international perspective, an awareness of transnational forces impinging on local decisions, and sophisticated methodological and theoretical frameworks.

The commodification of social services, as it is sometimes called, is abetted by a transfer of issues of citizenship to a forum which is no longer native in its scope but transnational; marked by intergovernmental structures, multinational corporate influence, and population changes (Ascoli & Ranci, 2002; Phillipson, 2006:202). There is another layer of complexity added by a worldwide tendency to view a number of social

Conclusion

73

issues through a medical lens (e.g., Kutchins & Kirk, 2003) and the insecurities experienced by the citizenry in general are without parallel in world history. What might be described as apodictic, self-evident truths of tradition tend to lose their currency and help demarcate generational and participatory categories from one another.

In the face of an unswerving drive to be players on the world's stage, enhance market share and survive economic rip-tides, nation-states must balance the demands of competing claimants—leaving them few options but to make hard choices. Not only do they have to adjudicate where to put scarce resources and which groups are deserving of protection or support, but few actions are indemnified against the next economic shortfall meaning they will have to review their priorities anew each time the economic tides turn. It has always been true that in times of plenty promises about solutions to societal woes are an easy pledge to make; during times of scarcity it is a different story and keeping even the best intentioned promises oftentimes creates real conflicts. Societal-level redefinitions of what is fair and just are a common means to solutions that do not always do well by citizens in need of assistance, undermining personal sense of security and identity as well as social solidarity (Powell, 2010).

An illustration of a macro-level problem may be helpful for thinking about the type of quandary involved. As nation-states undergo economic development via participation in global commerce, per capita incomes generally increase, never mind for the moment internal disparities, life expectancies increase, and demands for healthcare mount. Continued change and desires to remain viable in the global economy mean a country will face enduring challenges in providing social safety nets, medical interventions, or financing health care protections. To focus on just the health care issue: despite subsidized provisions for indigent citizens, most healthcare coverage around the world is linked to employment and economic productivity (workfare) and as employment is destabilized so, too, is healthcare. Needless to say, employment-based systems are costly, leading to cost shifting which also serves to grant license to employers to cut jobs and move production around to minimize the expense of doing business (ironically, economic reform in former socialist countries took the same direction, e.g., Chen,

2004). For those not covered by employment-based plans, subsidized coverage is oftentimes available but financed by taxes and premiums or by governmentally mandated insurance groups saddled with high expectations and expenditures. But social policies supportive of indigent care for those not involved in economically productive activities are often singled out as a cost sink and are among the first issues put on cost-cutting agenda (Jessop, 2002).

In order to comprehend the underpinning of certain forms of inequalities it is also important to examine some of the transformations that are altering people's lives. One post-modernist reality of the 21st century is the existence of a digital divide between those who have always known how to navigate in key-stroke technologies and those "ancients" who learned it later or not at all. Those who are comfortable with the technology have the world at their finger tips and no longer depend on local relationships or role models for solace or validation. The result is an indisputable social segmentation. Whatever norms of reciprocity had existed before are likely to falter and fray under the impact of interdicting worldviews in which the deep grammar of socialibility is no longer meaningful to those versed in the newer modes of activity. At the same time, there is an erosion of communities of like minds with shared representations cutting across society at large and fostering social solidarity. Instead they are replaced by segmented, smaller communities and a blurring of ways of knowing the world. Beck, Bonass and Lau (2003: 6) characterize the effects of technological innovation as "revolution through side effects" and suggest a deep-seeded societal segmentation is a likely upshot and should not be surprising. Addressing comparable consequences, Dasgupta (2006:159) phrased it succinctly: "globalization has thus created an identity crisis, since many are neither local nor global and are overloaded with changing stimuli…resulting in a 'don't care' attitude, commercial interactions among family members, a rise of individualism and a disequilibrium…."

Transnational private enterprises cannot be ignored as they are altering the landscape but they are not doing so single-handedly. It is fair to say there are both private and semi-public but non-governmental organizations (NGOs) involved. Multilateral NGOs are playing an especially crucial role and certainly a role that is influencing developing countries as they sort out their welfare regimes. For example, since the issuance of the Berg Report in 1981, the World Bank and the International Monetary Fund (IMF) have become major players on the world's stage oftentimes stipulating structural adjustments and preferred policies nation-states should adopt as a condition of support and in order to attract direct capital investments or other fiscal cooperation, including monetization. One illustration is that the World Bank began urging diminutions in pay-as-you-go (PAYG) pension provisions in favor of means-tested pensions and private provisions in the mid-1990s. The World Bank and the IMF have been staunch advocates for over three decades for broadly defined market-led welfare policies as a preferred alternative to un- or under-funded public welfare (Dembele, 2007; Wade, 2007). Encapsulating both the criticisms and the confluence of forces fueling such a movement, McMichael (2000) asserts that the drive for economic integration pays precious little attention to nation-building, national interests, or public sector regulatory control. As a consequence, even nonprofit, social enterprises tend to be "doing good badly" (Tekula, 2010).

MAKING SENSE OF SOCIAL WELFARE IN GLOBAL ARENA

Although there is a remarkable absence of consensus, social welfare is customarily taken to mean statutory governmental intervention designed to provide supportive services and resources to those in need. Right away one question that has to be addressed revolves around eligibility requirements and stipulations of entitlement. Such issues as gender are very much a part of the state, as are discussions of family responsibilities, and welfare policies. At the risk of extreme simplification, whether women are eligible for social benefits and services in their own rights or as members of a male-breadwinner family is an abiding question whenever welfare regimes are examined. By the same token, gender ideologies are very much an aspect of poverty, labor markets and other market experiences, or the myriad inequalities that cut across the life course and through virtually every facet of experience (Calasanti, 2001; Hatch, 2000; Sainsbury, 1994; 1996).

These same forces also affect lives in even more subtle ways beyond the realm of income, access or protection. Just one case in point out of scores of similar situations should suffice to illustrate our contention. It is fair to say that institutional arrangements and structural realignments have altered time and temporality as they have altered space and other normative aspects of life. Containing our focus to the issues discussed thus far; the ebb and flow of transnational capital markets operate around the clock and penetrates virtually every aspect of governmental policy and, accordingly, daily life. Analysts generally concur that there has been a compression of time in many corners of the world as they are pulled into global market flows (Powell, 2010). As should be fairly obvious, any attenuation of earlier subjective temporal reckoning requires a recalibration and re-integration as new templates are incorporated into mental models of what life is about. Analysts have asserted that globalization brings a dilation, fragmentation and acceleration of the sense of time unsettling to many (Lestienne, 2000). But, as with so many other aspects of globalization, the results do not settle on all people in equal fashion. For those who live along the margins of such change, feelings of being in-control and the clarity of their proleptic futures may be challenged as the pace, and types of engagements in their lives are restructured. Considered in a broader sense, temporal reorganization is also impacting event timing and thereby the shape of life, views of dependency, and definitions of personal worth. As normative perspectives on the shape of life are reformulated and/or personal functionality wanes, the chances increase that some subgroups within the population will lose track of their referential guidelines (Hill 2006).

In her insightful analysis of German pension provisions, Scheiwe (1994) brings a fresh perspective to discussion of how institutionalized welfare rules also structure temporality. She broadens the focus considerably in her examination of time politics and gendered times in legislation that grants standing to many market-related definitions of time and discounts others associated most frequently with women's roles outside the market or which result from discontinuous market-related activities deemed to be below time thresholds written into public welfare provisions. The gendered differentials in recognizing life's events, their timing and related circumstances serve to create essential inequalities in financial and other types of well-being. Time and temporality, sense of the future, and eligibility for entitlements impose structure on lives in ways that may not have been intended but are highly salient, nonetheless.

For the most part, a definition derived from the legendary Beveridge Report published in the midst of World War II in Britain has been utilized to identify and operationalize major features of the welfare state (Finer, 1999). Yet that formulation begs the question of whether that world and those circumstances still exist and how they may have been modified by post-industrial or globalizing influences. We would assert that a definition of social welfare must extend beyond questions of delivery to include its financing and function. Almost certainly the provision of non-governmental services through NGOs or volunteer agencies and programs should be included as well. Ambiguities not withstanding, it is hardly surprising that scholars looking at social welfare in a comparative focus have noted that there is a fairly direct correlation between national prosperity and percentage of GDP directed at supportive programs (Hill, 2006; Mabbett & Bolderson, 1999). However, within groups of nations (such as OECD, G-8, or G-20 countries) there are differences based on governmental types or economic developments and, we assert, in terms of underlying principles of moral economy that have shaped the formulation of welfare (Hendricks, 2005), whether that be public or private.

CONCLUSION

We have endeavored to illuminate the challenges to international social welfare in the broad context of global and post-industrial economy and public policy. We hope that it will provide researchers with a deeper understanding of the key issues of inequality and social justice with critical thinking about post-welfare state social policies (Esping-Andersen, 2002).

Inequality is an outstanding issue in the study of aging while globalization has widened its consequences such as planetary poverty and gender stratification. The potential reasons lie in the reformulation of economic power associated with burgeoning free-market economies and accompanying diffusion of instrumental rationality, standardization, commoditization, or secularism. In contrast with the economic downturn and global softening of labor markets which cry for greater social protection, the welfare state of the last century has been replaced by a competitive state of the 21st century, as a "non-sovereign power" mindful of its global positioning but less powerful in shaping daily life among social and economic forces.

REFERENCES

Achenbaum, A. W. 1978. *Old Age in the New Land*. Baltimore: John Hopkins University Press.

Age Concern England. 1997. *Age Matters: Report on a National Gallup Survey*. London: ACE.

Alcock, P. 1996. *Social Policy in Britain: Themes and Issues*. Basingstoke: Macmillan.

Allen, J. P. 2010 *Middle Egyptian: An Introduction to the Language and Culture of Hieroglyphs* Cambridge: Cambridge University Press.

Alley, D. E., Putney, N. M., Rice, M., (2009) 'The Increasing Use of Theory in Social Gerontology': 1990-2004 *Journals of Gerontology Series B – Psychological Sciences and Social Sciences* 65 (5): 583-590.

Annual World Wealth Report (2008). *12th Annual World Wealth Report*. New York: Merrill Lynch/Capgemini.

Appadurai, A. (2001). Grassroots globalization and the research imagination. In A. Appadurai (Ed.). *Globalization* (pp. 1-21). Durham, NC: Duke University Press.

Arber, S., and J. Ginn, eds. 1995. *Connecting Gender and Ageing: A Sociological Approach*. Milton Keynes, U.K.: Oxford University Press.

Arber, S., and J. Ginn. 1991. *Gender and Later Life: A Sociological Analysis of Resources and Constraints*. London: Sage.

References

Arias, A. O., & Logan, B. I. (2002) Conclusion: From globalization towards universalization in the twenty-first century. In B. I. Logan (Ed.). *Globalization, the third world state and poverty-alleviation in the twenty-first century* (pp. 197-202). Aldershot, UK: Ashgate.

Armstrong, D. 1983. *The Political Anatomy of the Body*. Cambridge: Cambridge University Press.

Armstrong, D. 1995 *Outline of Sociology as Applied to Medicine* London: Arnold Publishers.

Ascoli, U., & Ranci, C. (2002). The context of new social policies in Europe. In U. Ascoli & C. Ranci (Eds.). *Dilemmas of the welfare mix: The new structure of welfare in an era of privatization* (pp. 1-24). New York: Kluwer Academic/Plenum Publishers.

Atkinson, P. 1981 *The Clinical Experience: The Construction and Reconstruction of Medical Reality* Farnborough: Gower.

Baltes, B., and M. F. Baltes. 1990. *Successful Aging: Perspectives from the Behavioural Sciences*. New York: Cambridge University Press.

Baltes, M., and L. Carstersen. 1996. "The Process of Successful Ageing." *Ageing and Society* 16:397–422.

Bauman, Z. (1998) *Globalization; The human consequences*. New York: Columbia University Press.

Bauman, Z. 1992. *Imitations of Postmodernity*. London: Routledge.

———. 2001. *The Individualized Society*. Cambridge: Polity.

Beck, U. (1999). *World risk society*. Cambridge: Polity Press.

Beck, U. 1986. *Risikogesellschaft. Auf dem Weg in eine andere Moderne*. Frankfurt am Main: Suhrkamp.

———. 1992. *Risk Society: Towards a New Modernity*. London: Sage.

———. 1994. "The Reinvention of Politics: Towards a Theory of Reflexive Modernization." In *Reflexive Modernization: Politics, Tradition and Aesthetics in the Modern Social Order*, edited by U. Beck, A. Giddens, and S. Lash, 1–55. Stanford, Calif.: Stanford University Press.

———. 1998. *Democracy without Enemies, Polity*: Cambridge, UK.

———. 2005, *Power and Countervailing Power in the Global Age*. Cambridge: Polity.

References 81

Beck, U., Bonss, W. & Lau, C. (2003). "The theory of reflexive modernization: Problematic, hypotheses and research programme." *Theory, Culture & Society, 20,* 1-33.

Becker, H. S., Geer, B, Hughes, E. C. and Strauss, A. L. 1961 Boys in White: Student Culture in Medical School Chicago and London: University of Chicago Press.

Bengston, V., E. Burgess, and T. Parrot. 1997. "Theory, Explanation and a Third Generation of Theoretical Development in Social Gerontology." *Journal of Gerontology: Social Sciences* 52 (B): 72–88.

Bengston, V. L. and Lowenstein, A. (Eds.) (2004) *Global Aging and Challenges to Families.* New York: De Gruyter.

Bengtson V. L., Gans D., Putney N. M., Silverstein M., 2009 *Handbook of theories of aging.* New York: Springer.

Bengtson, V., and R. Schaie. 1999. *Handbook of Theories in Gerontology.* New York: Springer.

Bengtson, V. L. and Achenbaum, W. 1993, *The Changing Contract Across Generations*, Aldine De Gruyter: New York.

Bengtson, V. L., Giarrusso, R., Silverstein, M., and Wang, H. (2000), Families and Intergenerational Relationships in Aging Societies, *Hallym International Journal of Aging*, Vol. 2, No. 1, pp. 3-10.

Best, F. 1980. *Flexible Life Scheduling.* New York: Praeger.

BGOP, *Better Government of Older People* (2000), Better Government for Older People, BGOP: Wolverhampton, UK.

Biggs, S. 1993. *Understanding Ageing.* Milton Keynes, U.K.: Oxford University Press.

———. 1996. "A Family Concern: Elder Abuse in British Social Policy." *Critical Social Policy* 16 (2): 63–88.

———. 1999. *The Mature Imagination.* Milton Keynes, U.K.: Oxford University Press.

———. 2001, Toward Critical Narrativity: Stories of Aging in Contemporary Social Policy, *Journal of Aging Studies*, Vol. 15, pp. 1-14.

82 *References*

Biggs, S., and J. L. Powell. 2000. "Surveillance and Elder Abuse: The Rationalities and Technologies of Community Care." *Journal of Contemporary Health* 4 (1): 43–49.

———. 2001. "A Foucauldian Analysis of Old Age and the Power of Social Welfare." *Journal of Aging & Social Policy* 12 (2): 93–111.

———. 2002. "Older People and Family Policy: A Critical Narrative." In *International Perspectives on the Family*, edited by V. Bengston and A. Lowenstein. Thousand Oaks, Calif.: Pine Forge Press.

Biggs, S., Estes, C., and Phillipson, C. 2003, *Social Theory, Social Policy and Ageing*, Open University Press: Buckingham, UK.

Biggs, S.; Phillipson, C., and Kingston, P. 1995, *Elder Abuse in Perspective*, Open University Press: Buckingham, UK.

BJF, Beth Johnson Foundation 1999, *Intergenerational Programmes*, BJF: Stoke, UK.

Blaikie, A. 1999. *Ageing and Popular Culture*. Cambridge: Cambridge University Press.

Blair, T. 1996, *New Britain: My Vision of a Young Country*, Fourth Estate: London.

Blecher, M. (1997), *China against the Tides: Restructuring through Revolution, Radicalism and Reform*, London: Pinter.

Boaz, A., Hayden, C., and Bernard, M. 1999, Attitudes and Aspiriations of Older People. *DSS Research Report, No. 101*, CDS: London.

Bond, J., and P. Coleman. 1990. *Ageing in Society*. London: Sage.

Bone, M. 1996. *Trends in Dependency among Older People in England*. London: Office of Population and Census Statistics.

Boneham, M., and K. Blakemore. 1994. *Age, Race and Ethnicity*. Buckingham: Oxford University Press.

Bornat, J., et al. eds. 1993. *Community Care: A Reader*. Milton Keynes, U.K.: Oxford University Press.

Bornat, J.; Dimmock, B.; Jones, D., and Peace, S. (1999), Stepfamilies and Older People, *Ageing and Society*, Vol. 19, No. 2, pp. 239-62.

Bowl, R. 1986. "Social Work with Old People." In *Ageing and Social Policy*, edited by C. Phillipson and A. Walker. London: Gower.

References 83

Braidotti, R. 1994. *Nomadic Subjects. Embodiment and Sexual Difference in Contemporary Feminist Theory.* New York: Columbia University Press.

Building blocks (2004) *Africa-wide briefing notes – supporting older carers,* HIV AIDS Alliance and HelpAge International.

Burchell, G. 1993. "Liberal Government and the Techniques of the Self." *Economy and Society* 22 (3): 267–82.

Burchell, G., et al. 1991. *The Foucault Effect: Studies in Governmentality.* Hemel Hempstead: Harvester Wheatsheaf.

Bury, M. 1995. "Ageing, Gender and Sociological Theory." In *Connecting Gender and Ageing: A Sociological Approach,* edited by S. Arber and J. Ginn. Milton Keynes, U.K.: Oxford University Press.

Butler, J. 1987. *Bodies that Matter on the Discursive Limits of "Sex."* Oxford: Clarendon.

Bytheway, B. 1993. "Ageing and Biography: The Letters of Bernard and Mary Berenson." *Sociology* 27 (1): 153–65.

Bytheway, B., and J. Johnson. 1998. "The Sight of Age." In *The Body in Everyday Life,* edited by S. Nettleton and J. Watson, 62–85.

Bytheway, W. 1995. *Ageism.* Milton Keynes, U.K.: Oxford University Press.

Cabinet Office UK. 1998. *Better Government for Older People.* London: H.M.S.O.

Calasanti, T. M. (2001). *Gender, social inequalities and aging.* Walnut Creek, CA: AltaMira.

Calasanti, T. M. 1996. "Incorporating Diversity: Meaning, Levels of Research, and Implications for Theory." *The Gerontologist* 36 (2): 147–56.

Carmel, S.; Morse, C. A., and Torres-Gil, F. M. 2007, *Lessons on Aging from Three Nations,* Baywood: New York.

Carr-Saunders, A. M. and Wilson, P. A. 1933 *The Professions* London: The Clarendon Press.

Carter, K. C. 1991 The development of Pasteur's concept of disease: causation and the emergence of specific causes in nineteenth century medicine *Bulletin of the History of Medicine* 2: 528-548.

References

Cassel, E. J. 1991. *The Nature of Suffering and the Goals of Medicine*. New York: Oxford University Press.

Castel, R. 1991. "From Dangerousness to Risk." In *The Foucault Effect: Studies in Governmentality*, edited by G. Burchell, C. Gordon, and P. Miller. London: Harvester Wheatsheaf: 281–98.

Castells, M. (2000). *The rise of the network society: The information age: Economy, society and culture, Volume 1* (2nd edition). Oxford, UK: Blackwell.

Chadwick, J and Mann, W. N. 1950 *The Medical Works of Hippocrates* Oxford: Blackwell.

Chamberlayne, P. and King, A. 2000, *Cultures of Care*, Policy Press: London.

Chambre, S. M. 1993, Volunteerism by Elders: Past Traditions and Future Prospects, *The Gerontologist*, Vol. 33, pp. 221-28.

Chau, W. F. 1995. "Experts, Networks and Inscriptions in the Fabrication of Accounting Images." *Accounting Organisations and Society* 20 (2/3): 111–45.

Chen, S and Powell, J. L. (2011) *Aging in Perspective and the Case of China*. Nova Science: New York.

Chen, S and Powell, J. L. (Eds.) *Aging in Perspective and the Case of China*, Nova Science: New York.

Chen, S. (2004). *Public Policy and Development Strategy: Theoretical, Comparative, and Historical Perspectives Illustrated with the Case of the Chinese State*. Dubuque, IA: Kendall/Hunt Publishing.

Chen, S., & Ravallion, M. (2007). The Changing Profile of Poverty in the World. *2020 FOCUS BRIEF on the World's Poor and Hungry People*. Washington, D.C.: International Food Policy Research Institute.

Chen, Y. P., & Turner, J. (2006). Economic resources: Implications for aging policy in Asia. In H. Yoon & J. Hendricks (Eds.). *Handbook of Asian Aging* (pp. 67-90). Amityville, NY: Baywood.

China Daily (2004), "*Tailoring Health Care Policies for the Elderly*," April 15th 2004.

References

Christian, B. 1996. "The Race for Theory." In *Radically Speaking: Feminism Reclaimed*, edited by D. Bell and R. Klein. London: Zed Books.

Chudacoff, H. 1989. *How Old Are You?* Princeton, N.J.: Princeton University Press.

Clark, G. (2007). *A farewell to alms: A brief economic history of the world*. Princeton, NJ: Princeton University Press.

Cloke, P., Johnsen, S., and May, J. 2006 Ethical citizenship? *Volunteers and the ethics of providing services for homeless people Geoforum* 38(6): 1089-1101.

Clough, R. 1988. *Practice, Politics and Power in Social Service Departments*. Aldershot, U.K.: Gower.

Clough, R., and C. Hadley. 1996. *Care in Chaos*. London: Cassel.

Cohen, S. 1985. *Visions of Social Control*. Cambridge: Polity.

Cole, T., D. Van Tassel, and R. Kastenbaum. 1992. *Handbook of the Humanities and Aging*. New York: Springer.

Connor, S. 1989. *Postmodernist Culture*. Oxford: Basil Blackwell.

Conrad, S. 1992. "Old Age in the Modern and Postmodern Western World." In *Handbook of the Humanities and Aging*, edited by T. Cole. New York: Springer Publishing Company.

Cook, I. G. 2001. *A Human Geography of China*. London: Curzon.

Cook, I. G., and G. Murray. 2000. *China's Third Revolution: Tensions in the Transition to Post-Communism*. London: Curzon.

Cook, I. G., and J. L. Powell. 2003. "Active Aging in China." *Journal of Social Sciences and Humanities* 26 (2): 1–10.

Cook, I. G. and Murray, G. (2001), *China's Third Revolution: Tensions in the Transition to Post-Communism*, Curzon: London.

Cook, I. G. and Powell, J. L. (2007) *New Perspectives on China and Aging*. Nova Science: New York.

Copeman, W. S. C. 1960 *Doctors and Disease in Tudor Times* London: Dawson and Sons.

Cousins, M., and A. Hussain. 1984. *Michel Foucault*. London: Macmillan.

Cumming, E., and W. Henry. 1961. *Growing Old: The Process of Disengagement*. New York: Basic Books.

86 *References*

Dalley, G. 1988. *Ideologies of Caring*. London: Macmillan.

Dallmayer, F. (2005). *Small Wonder: Global Power and its Discontents*. Lanham, MD: Rowman & Littlefield.

Dasgupta, S. (2006). Globalization and its future shock. In S. Dasgupta & R. Kiely (Eds.), *Globalization and after* (pp. 143-183). Thousand Oaks, CA: Sage.

Davidson, A. 1986. "Archaeology, Genealogy, Ethics." In *Foucault: A Critical Reader*, edited by D. Hoy. Oxford: Basil Blackwell.

De Beauvoir, S. 1979, *Old Age*, Penguin: London.

Deacon, B., Hulse, M., & Stubbs, P. (1997). *Global social policy: International organizations and the future of welfare*. Thousand Oaks, CA: Sage.

Deakin, N. 1996. "The Devil's in the Detail: Some Reflections on Contracting for Social Care." *Social Policy and Administration* 30 (1): 20–38.

Delanty, G. 1999. *Social Science: Beyond Constructivism*. London: Sage.

Dembele, D. M. (2007). The International Monetary Fund and the World Bank in Africa: A disastrous record. In V. Navarro (Ed.), *Neoliberalism, globalization and inequalities: Consequences for health and quality of life* (pp. 369-377). Amityville, NY: Baywood.

Derrida, J. 1978. *Writing and Difference*. Chicago: University of Chicago Press.

Donzelot, J. 1979. *The Policing of Families*. London: Hutchinson.

———. 1988. "The Promotion of the Social." *Economy and Society* 17 (3): 395–427.

Douglas, M. 1985. *Risk Acceptability According to the Social Sciences*. New York: Sage.

Dreyer, J. T. (1996), *China's Political System: Modernization and Tradition*, 2nd Edition, London: Macmillan.

Dreyfus, H., and P. Rabinow. 1983. *Michel Foucault: Beyond Hermeneutics*, London: Tavistock.

DSS, Department of Social Security 1998, *Building a Better Britain for Older People,* HMSO: London.

Du Gay, P. 1996. *Consumption and Identity*. London: Sage.

References 87

Du, P. and Tu, P. (2000) 'Population Ageing and Old Age Security,' chapter in in Peng X. and Guo Z. (eds), *The Changing Population of China*, Oxford: Blackwell, pp. 77-90.

Du, P. and Tu, P. (2000), Population Ageing and Old-Age Security, in W. Z. Peng and Z. G. Guo (eds.), *The Changing Population of China*, Blackwell: Oxford, UK.

Du, P., and P. Tu. 2000. "Population Ageing and Old Age Security." In *The Changing Population of China*, edited by X. Peng and Z. Guo, 77–90. Oxford: Blackwell.

Duckworth, L. 2001, *Grandparents Who Bring Up Children Need More Help*, Independent, September 13.

Elder, G. 1977. *The Alienated: Growing Old Today*. London: Writers and Readers Publishing Co-operative.

Epstein, H. (2001) 'Time of Indifference,' *New York Review of Books,* April 12, pp. 33-38.

Erikson, E. 1980. *Identity and the Life Cycle: A Re-issue*. New York: W. W. Norton.

Esping-Andersen, G. (1990). *Three worlds of welfare capitalism.* Cambridge: Polity Press.

Esping-Andersen, G. (2002). *Why we need a new welfare state*. Oxford: Oxford University Press.

Estes, C. 1979. *The Aging Enterprise*. San Francisco: Jossey-Bass.

Estes, C. and Associates (2001) *Social Policy and Aging*. Sage: Thousand Oaks.

Estes, C., and Associates. 2001. *Social Policy and Aging*. Thousand Oaks, Calif.: Sage.

Estes, C., and E. A. Binney. 1989. "The Biomedicalization of Aging: Dangers and Dilemmas." *The Gerontologist* 29 (5): 587–96.

Estes, C., Biggs, S and Phillipson, C. (2003) *Social Policy, Social Theory and Ageing* OUP: Maidenhead.

Estes, C., Biggs, S and Phillipson, C. (2003) *Social Theory, Social Policy and Ageing*. Open University Press: Milton Keynes.

References

Estes, C., J. Swan, and L. Gerard. 1982. "Dominant and Competing Paradigms in Gerontology: Towards a Political Economy of Ageing." *Ageing and Society* 12:151–64.

Estes, C., S. Biggs, and C. Phillipson. 2003. *Social Theory, Social Policy and Ageing*. Milton Keynes, U.K.: Oxford University Press.

Ewald, F. 1993. "Two Infinities of Risk." In *The Politics of Everyday Fear*, edited by B. Massumi. Minneapolis: University of Minnesota Press.

Fattah, E. A., and V. F. Sacco. 1989. *Crime and Victimisation of the Elderly*. New York: Springer.

Featherstone, M., and A. Wernick. 1995. *Images of Ageing*. London: Routledge.

Featherstone, M., and M. Hepworth. 1993. "Images in Ageing." In *Ageing in Society*, edited by J. Bond, P. Coleman, and S. Peace. London: Sage.

Federal Reserve Bank of Kansas City (2004) *Global Demographic Change: Economic Impacts and Policy Challenges. Symposium proceedings*. August 26–28, 2004. Available at: http://www.kc.frb.org/Publicat/sympos/2004/sym04prg.htm.

Fennell, G., et al. 1988. *Sociology of Age*. Buckingham: Oxford University Press.

Finch, J. 1986. "Age." In *Key Variables in Social Investigation*, edited by R. Burgess. London: Routledge & Kegan Paul.

Finch, J. and Mason, J. 1993, *Negotiating Family Responsibilities*, Routledge: London.

Finer, C. (1999). Trends and developments in welfare states. In J. Clasen (Ed.). *Comparative social policy: Concepts, theories and methods* (pp. 15-33). Oxford: Blackwell.

Flynn, R. 1992. *Structures of Control in Health Management*. London: Routledge.

———. 2002. "Clinical Governance and Governmentality." *Health, Risk & Society* 4 (2): 155–73.

Fortes, M. 1984. "Age, Generation and Social Structure." In *Age and Anthropological Theory*, edited by D. Kertzer and J. Keith. London: Cornell University Press.

Foucault, M. (1972), *The Archeology of Knowledge*, Tavistock: London.

References

89

Foucault, M. (1978). *The history of sexuality*. New York: Pantheon Books.

Foucault, M. 1967. *Madness and Civilisation*. London: Tavistock.

———. 1972. *The Archaeology of Knowledge*. London: Tavistock.

———. 1973. *The Birth of the Clinic*. London: Routledge.

———. 1976. *The History of Sexuality*. Harmondsworth: Penguin.

———. 1977. *Discipline and Punish*. London: Tavistock.

———. 1978. "Governmentality." In *The Foucault Effect*, edited by G. Burchell, C. Gordon, and P. Miller 1991.

———. 1980. *Power/Knowledge: Selected Interviews and Other Writings, 1972–1977*. New York: Pantheon.

———. 1982. "The Subject of Power." In *Michel Foucault: Beyond Structuralism and Hermeneutics*, edited by H. Dreyfus and P. Rabinow. Brighton, U.K.: Harvester.

———. 1988. "Technologies of the Self." In *Technologies of the Self*, edited by L. H. Martin, et al. London: Tavistock.

Frank, A. W. 1990. "Bringing Bodies Back In: A Decade Review." *Theory, Culture & Society* 7 (1): 131–62.

———. 1991. "For a Sociology of the Body: An Analytical Review." In *The Body Social Processes and Cultural Theory*, edited by M. Featherstone, M. Hepworth, and B. Turner. London: Sage.

———. 1996. *The Wounded Storyteller: Body, Illness and Ethics*. Chicago: University of Chicago Press.

Frank, A. W. (1998), Stories of Illness as Care of the Self: A Foucauldian Dialogue, *Health*, Vol. 2, No. 3, pp. 329-48.

Fraser, N. (2005). Transnationalizing the public sphere. In M. Pensky (Ed.), *Globalizing Critical Theory* (pp. 37-47). Lanham, MD: Rowman & Littlefield.

Fraser, N. 1987. "Women, Welfare and the Politics of Need Interpretation." *Hytapia: A Journal of Feminist Philosophy* 2:102–21.

Freidenberg, J. 2000, *Growing Old in EL Barrio*, New York University Press: New York.

Freund, P. 1988. "Bringing Society into the Body: Understanding Socialized Human Nature." *Theory and Society* 17:839–64.

Friedan, B. 1993. *The Fountain of Age*. London: Cape Books.

90 *References*

Fullmer, E. M. 1995. "Challenging Biases against Families of Older Gays and Lesbians." In Streng*thening Aging Families: Diversity in Practice and Policy,* edited by G. C. Smith, S. S. Tobin, et al. 99–119. Thousand Oaks, Calif.: Sage.

Garland, D. 1985. *Punishment and Welfare.* Aldershot, U.K.: Gower.

Gavrilov, L and Gavrilova, N (1991) *The Biology of Life Span: A Quantitative Approach.* New York: Harwood Academic Publisher.

Geertz, C. (1973). *The Interpretation of Cultures.* New York: Basic Books.

George, L. 1995. "The Last Half-Century of Aging Research—and Thoughts for the Future." *Journal of Gerontology: Social Sciences* 50 (B) (1): 1–3.

Giddens A. (1990). *The Consequences of Modernity.* Cambridge: Polity Press.

Giddens, A (1993) *Sociology.* Cambridge Polity Press.

Giddens, A. 1987. *Social Theory and Modern Sociology.* Cambridge: Polity.

———. 1990. *The Consequences of Modernit.* Cambridge: Polity.

———. 1991. *Modernity and Self- Identity: Self and Society in the Late Modern Age.* Cambridge: Polity.

———. 1998. *The Third Way, Polity*: Cambridge.

Gilleard, C and Higgs, P. (2001). *Cultures of Aging.* London: Prentice Hall.

Girrard, I. and Ogg, J. (1998), *Grand-parenting in France and England, paper presented to the British Society of Gerntology*, Sheffield, UK.

Gittens, C. 1997. *The Pursuit of Beauty.* London: NPG.

Gordon, C. 1991. "Governmental Rationality: An Introduction." In *The Foucault Effect*, edited by G. Burchell, C. Gordon, and P. Miller, 1–51. Chicago: Chicago University Press.

Government of China (2002), *China Statistical Yearbook 2002*, China Statistics Press: Beijing.

Government of China (2002), *China Statistical Yearbook 2002*, China Statistics Press: Beijing.

Granovetter, M. 1985. "Economic Action and Social Structure—The Problem of Embeddedness." *American Journal of Sociology* 91 (3): 481–510.

References

———. 1992. "Economic Institutions as Social Constructions," *Acta Sociologica* 25 (3): 3–11.

Gray, J. 1995, *Enlightenment's Wake*, Routledge: London.

Greenblatt, S. 1980. *Renaissance Self–Fashioning: From More to Shakespeare*. Chicago: Chicago University Press.

Grosz, E. 1994. *Volitile Bodies*. Bloomington: Indiana University Press.

Gruber J., and Wise D. A., (eds.) (1999) *Social Security and Retirement around the World*. Chicago, IL: University of Chicago Press, 1999.

Gruber J., and Wise D. A., (eds.) (2004) *Social Security Programs and Retirement around the World. Micro Estimation*. Chicago, IL: University of Chicago Press.

Guardian-ICM Poll 2001, *Grandparenting and Retirement Activities*, ICM: London.

Gubrium, J. F. (1992), *Out of Control: Family Therapy and Domestic Disorder*, Sage: Thousand Oaks, CA.

Gutting, G., ed. 1994. *The Cambridge Companion to Foucault*. Cambridge: Cambridge University Press.

Habermas, J. 1981. *The Theory of Communicative Action*. London: Beacon Press.

———. 1984. *The Philosophical Discourse of Modernity*. Cambridge: Polity.

———. 1992. *Postmetaphysical Thinking*. Cambridge: Polity.

Hacking, I. 1990. *The Taming of Chance*. Cambridge: Cambridge University Press.

Hadley, R. and Clough, R. (1996), *Care in Chaos*, Continuum International: New York.

Hall, S., ed. 1992. *Modernity and Its Futures*. Cambridge: Polity.

Hallam, E., J. Hockey, and G. Howarth. 1999. *Beyond the Body: Death and Social Identity*. London: Routledge.

Hansson, A. (1996), *Chinese Outcasts: Discrimination and Emancipation in Late Imperial China*, E. J. Brill: Leiden, The Netherlands.

Haraway, D. 1991. *Simians, Cyborgs and Women*. London: Free Association Books.

References

Hardill, I. and Baines, S. and 6, P., 2007 Volunteering for all? Explaining patterns of volunteering and identifying strategies to promote it, *Policy and Politics*. 35 (3): 395-412.

Hargrave, T. and Anderson, W. 1992, *Finishing Well: Aging and Reparation in the Intergenerational Family,* Brunner and Mazel: New York.

Harper, S. (1994), China's Population: Prospects and Policies, in D. Dwyer (ed.), *China: The Next Decades, Longman Scientific and Technical*: Harlow, UK.

Harper, S. 1997. "Constructing Later Life/Constructing the Body: Some Thoughts from Feminist Theory." In *Critical Approaches to Ageing and Later Life*, edited by A. Jamieson, S. Harper, and C. Victor, 160–71. Buckingham: Open University Press.

Harper, S., and G. Laws. 1995. "Rethinking the Geography of Ageing." *Progress in Human Geography* 19 (2): 199–221.

Hart, G. (2002). *Disabling globalization: Places of power in post-apartheid South Africa.* Berkeley, CA: University of California Press.

Hatch, L. R. (2000). *Beyond gender differences.* Amityville, NY: Baywood.

Hayden, C., Boaz, A., and Taylor, F. (1999), Attitudes and Aspirations of Older People: A Qualitative Study, *DSS Research Report*, No. 102, CDS, London.

Heidegger, M. (1971), *Poetry, Language, Thought, Harper and Row*: New York.

Help the Age International (2000) *The Mark of a Noble Society.* London: HelpAge International.

Hendricks, J. (2005). Moral economy and aging. In M. L. Johnson (Ed.). *Cambridge handbook of age and ageing* (pp. 510-517). Cambridge: Cambridge University Press.

Hermalin A, (ed.) (2002) *The Well-Being of the Elderly in Asia: A Four-Country Comparative Study*. Ann Arbor, MI: University of Michigan Press.

Hewitt, M. 1983. "Bio-politics and Social Policy: Foucault's Account of Welfare." *Theory, Culture and Society* 2 (1): 67–84.

Hill, M. (2006). *Social policy in the modern world.* Oxford: Blackwell.

Hirst, P. 1981. "The Genesis of the Social." *Politics and Power* 3:67–82.

References

93

Hockey, J. and A. James. 1993. *Growing Up and Growing Old: Ageing and Dependency in the Life Course*, London: Sage.

Holloway, T. 1966 *The Apothecaries Act, 1815: A Reinterpretation* (part 1) Medical History 10th July 1966, 107-29.

Holstein, J. and Gubrium, J. 2000, *The Self We Live By*, Oxford University Press: Oxford, UK.

Holtzman, R. A. (1997) *A World Bank Perspective on Pension Reform.* Paper prepared for the joint ILO-OECD Workshop on the Development and Reform of Pension Schemes, Paris, December.

Hoogvelt, A. (1997). *Globalization and the postcolonial world: The new political economy of development.* Baltimore, MD: Johns Hopkins University Press.

Howe, A. 1994. *Punish and Critique: Towards a Feminist Analysis of Penality.* London: Routledge.

Howe, D. 1992. "Child Abuse and the Bureacratization of Social Work." *Sociological Review* 40 (3): 491–505.

Hudson, J., & Lowe, S. (2004). *Understanding the policy process: Analysing Welfare policy and practice.* Bristol, UK: Polity Press.

Hughes, B. 1995. *Older People and Community Care: Critical Theory and Practice.* Milton Keynes, U.K.: Oxford University Press.

Ignatieff, M. 1978. *A Just Measure of Pain.* London: Macmillan.

Ingleby, D. 1985. "Professionals as Socialisers: The 'Psy' Complex." In *Research in Law, Deviance and Social Control*, edited by A. Scully and S. Spitzer, 7.

International Monetary Fund. *The Economics of Demographics. Finance and Development. September* (2006);43(3). Available at: http://www.imf.org/external/pubs/ft/fandd/2006/09/.

Irvine, E. 1954. "Research into Problem Families." *British Journal of Psychiatric Social Work* 9 (Spring).

Isay, R. A. 1996. Becoming Gay: *The Journey to Self-acceptance.* New York: Pantheon Books.

Itzin, C. 1986. "Ageism Awareness Training: A Model for Group Work." In *Dependency and Interdependency in Old Age: Theoretical Perspectives* and *Policy Alternatives*, edited by C. Phillipson, M. Bernard, and P. Strang. London: Croom Helm.

Izuhara, M. 2000, *Family Change and Housing in Postwar Japanese Society*, Ashgate: Aldershot, UK.

Jameson, F. 1991. *Postmodernism, or, the Cultural Logic of Late Capitalism*. London: Verso.

Jefferys, M., and P. Thane. 1989. "An Ageing Society and Ageing People." In *Growing Old in the Twentieth Century*, edited by M. Jefferys. London: Routledge.

Jessop, B. (2002). *The future of the capitalist state*. Bristol, UK: Polity Press.

Jewson, N. D. 1974 *Medical Knowledge and the Patronage System in Eighteenth Century England Sociology* 8: 369-85.

Jewson, N. D. 1976 *The Disappearance of the Sick-Man from the Medical Cosmology Sociology*, 10: 225-44.

Johnson, T J 1977 *Professions in the Cass Structure in Scase*, R (editor) Class Cleavage and Control Allen and Unwin.

Johnson, T. 1995. "Governmentality and the Institutionalisation of Expertise." In *Health Professions and the State in Europe*, edited by G. Larkin, et al. London: Routledge.

Johnson, T. J. 1972 *Professions and Power* MacMillian Press Ltd.

Jones, C. 1983. *State Social Work and the Working* Class. London: Macmillan.

Kalish, R. 1979. "The New Ageism and the Failure Models: A Polemic." *The Gerontologist* 19 (4).

Kastenbaum, R. 1993. "Encrusted Elders." In *Voices & Visions of Aging*, edited by T. Cole. New York: Springer.

Katz, S. (1996), *Disciplining Old Age: The Formation of Gerontological Knowledge,* The University Press of Virginia: Charlottesville, VA.

―――. 1999. "Lifecourse, Lifestyle and Postmodern Culture: Corporate Representations of Later Life," *paper presented at Restructuring Work and the Lifecourse: An International Symposium, Institute of Human Development*, University of Toronto.

―――. 1999. Busy Bodies: Activity, Aging, and the Management of Everyday Life, *Journal of Aging Studies*, Vol. 14, No. 2, pp. 135-52.

References

——. 2000. "Busy Bodies: Activity, Aging and the Management of Everyday Life." *Journal of Aging Studies* 14 (2): 135–52.

Katz, S. (2000), Busy Bodies: Activity, Aging and the Management of Everyday Life, *Journal of Aging Studies*, Vol. 14, No. 2, pp. 135-52.

Kearney, M. (1995). The local and the global: The anthropology of globalization and transnationalism. *Annual Review of Anthropology*, 24: 547-565.

Kennedy, G. 1990, College Students Expectations of Grandparent and Grandchild Role Behaviours, *The Gerontologist*, Vol. 30, No. 1, pp. 43-48.

Kennett, P. (2001). *Comparative social policy*. Buckingham: Open University Press.

Kenyon, G., Ruth, J., and Mader, W. 1999, Elements of a Narrative Gerontology, in V. Bengtson and K. Schaie (eds.), *Handbook of Theories of Ageing*, Springer: New York.

Kim, S., and Lee, J. W., (2007), "Demographic changes, saving and current account in East Asia," *Asian Economic Papers*, 6(2).

King, H 2001 Greek and Roman Medicine. London: Bristol Classical Press.

Kinsella K., and Velkoff V. A. (2001) *An Aging World: 2001*. Washington, DC: National Institute on Aging and U.S. Census Bureau.

Kivnick, H. 1988, Grandparenthood, Life Review and Psychosocial Development, *Journal of Gerontological Social Work*, Vol. 12, No. 3, pp. 63-82.

Krug, E. G., (2002), *World Report on Violence and Health*, World Health Organization: Geneva, Switzerland.

Kunkel, S., and L. Morgan. 1999. *Aging: The Social Context*. New York: Pine Forge.

Kutchins, H., & Kirk, S. A. (2003). *Making Us Crazy - DSM: The Psychiatric Bible and the Creation of Mental Disorders*. New York: Free Press.

Land, H. 1999, *The Changing Worlds of Work and Families*, Open University Press: Buckingham, UK.

Lane, J. 1985 *The Role of Apprenticeship in Eighteenth Century Medial Education in England*. in Bynum W. F and Porter, R (1985, editors)

References

William Hunter and the Eighteenth Century Medical World Cambridge University Press.

Leonard, P. 1997. *Postmodern Welfare*. London: Sage.

Lestienne, R. (2000). Time and globalization: does the emergence of a global identity entail a loss of individualities. *Time and Society, 9,* 289-291.

Lindeman, M. (1999) *Medicine and Society in Early Modern Europe Cambridge*: Cambridge University Press.

Liu, J. and Lin, F. (2000), *Long-Term Effect of China's Family Planning.*

Liu, W. (1973), 'Chinese Society: Stratification, Minorities, and the Family,' Chapter 26 in Wu, Y. L. (ed.), *China: A Handbook*, Newton Abbot, Devon, UK: David & Charles.

Loewe, M. (1973), *Everyday Life in Early Imperial China*, London: Carousel.

Longino, C. F. (1994). 'Pressure from our aging population will broaden our understanding of medicine.' *Academic Medicine, 72* (10), 841-847.

Longino, C. F., and J. L. Powell. 2004. "Embodiment and the Study of Aging." In *The Body in Human Inquiry: Interdisciplinary Explorations of Embodiment*, edited by V. Berdayes. New York: Hampton Press.

Lopez A. D., Mathers C. D., Ezzati M., Jamison D. T., and Murray C. J. L., (eds.) (2006) *Global Burden of Disease and Risk Factors.* Washington, DC: The World Bank Group.

Lubove, R. 1966. "Social Work and the Life of the Poor." *The Nation*, 23 May, 609–11.

Luhmann, N. 1993. *Risk: A Sociological Theory*. Berlin: Walter de Gruyter.

Lupton, D. 1999. *Risk*. New York: Routledge.

Lyotard, J. F. 1984. *The Postmodern Condition: A Report on Knowledge*. Manchester, U.K.: Manchester University Press.

Mabbett, D., & Bolderson, H. (1999). Theories and methods in comparative social policy. In J. Clasen (Ed.). *Comparative social policy: Concepts, theories and methods* (pp. 34-56). Oxford: Blackwell.

Mabbett, D., & Bolderson, H. (1999). Theories and methods in comparative social policy. In J. Clasen (Ed.). *Comparative social policy: Concepts, theories and methods* (pp. 34-56). Oxford: Blackwell.

References

Manton, K. G. and Gu X. (2001) Changes in the prevalence of chronic disability in the United States black and nonblack population above age 65 from 1982 to 1999. *Proceedings of the National Academy of Sciences* 98;6354-6359.

Massumi, B., ed. 1993. *The Politics of Everyday Fear*. Minneapolis: University of Minnesota Press.

May, T. 1996. *Situating Social Theory*. Milton Keynes, U.K.: Oxford University Press.

May, T. and Powell, J. L. (2008) *Situating Social Theory 2*. McGraw Hill: Maidenhead Organisation for Economic Cooperation and Development (OECD) Directorate for Employment, Labour and Social Affairs. (2007) *Disability Trends among Elderly People: Re-Assessing the Evidence in 12 OECD Countries* (Interim Report). Paris, France: OECD.

McAdams, D. 1993. *The Stories We Live By*. New York: Morrow.

McLennan, G. 1992. "The Enlightenment Project Revisited." In *Modernity and Its Futures*, edited by S. Hall, D. Held, and T. McGrew. Cambridge: Polity.

McLeod, J. 1997, *Narrative and Psychotherapy*, Sage: London.

McMichael, P. (2000). *Development and social change*. Thousand Oaks, CA: Pine Forge Press.

Miller, J. 1993. *The Passion of Michel Foucault*. New York: Simon & Schuster.

Mills, C. W. 1959. *The Sociological Imagination*. London: Penguin.

Mills, T. 1999, When Grandchildren Grow Up, *Journal of Aging Studies*, Vol. 13, No. 2, pp. 219-39.

Minkler, M. 1999, Intergenerational Households Headed by Grandparents: Con-texts, Realities and Implications for Policy, *Journal of Aging Studies*, Vol. 13, No. 2, pp. 199-218.

Minkler, M., and C. Estes, eds. 1998. *Critical Gerontology: Perspectives from Political and Moral Economy*. New York: Baywood.

Mishra, R. (1999). *Globalization and the welfare state*. Cheltenham, UK: Edward Elgar.

References

Mölling, G. 2001. "The Nature of Trust: From George Simmel to a Theory of Expectation, Interpretation and Suspension." *Sociology* 35 (2): 403–20.

Moody, H. 1998. *Aging, Concepts and Controversies*. Thousand Oaks, Calif.: Pine Forge Press, Sage.

Morris, D. B. 1991. *The Culture of Pain*. London: University of California Press.

———. 1998. *Illness and Culture in the Postmodern Age*. London: University of California Press.

Mouzelis, N. 1991. *Back to Sociological Theory*. London: Macmillan.

Muirhead-Little, E. (1932) *The History of the British Medical Association: 1832 to 1932*. London: BMA Publishing.

Murphy, J. W., and C. F. Longino Jr. 1997. "Reason, the Lifeworld, and Appropriate Intervention." *Journal of Applied Gerontology* 16 (2): 149–51.

Murray, G. (1998), *China: The Next Superpower*, China Library: London.

Murray, G. (2004), *China's Population Control Policy: A Socio-Economic Reassessment*, PhD thesis, Liverpool John Moores University: Liverpool, UK.

Navarro, V. (2007). Neoliberalism as a class ideology; or, the political causes of the growth of inequalities. In V. Navarro (Ed.), *Neoliberalism, globalization and inequalities: Consequences for health and quality of life* (pp. 9-23). Amityville, NY: Baywood.

Neugarten, B. L. 1974. "Age Groups in American Society and the Rise of the Young-old." *Annals of the American Academy of Political and Social Sciences* 415: 187–98.

Neugarten, D., ed. 1996. *The Meanings of Age*. Chicago: University of Chicago Press.

O'Malley, C. D. 1970 *The History of Medical Education Berkley and Los Angeles*.

Oberg, P., and L. Tornstam. 1999. "Body Images among Men and Women of Different Ages." *Ageing and Society* 19:645–58.

Pain, R. 2003. "Old Age and Victimisation." In *Victimisation, Theory, Research and Policy*, edited by P. Davis, et al. London: Macmillan.

References
99

Parry, N and Parry, J. 1976 *The Rise of The Medical Profession: A Study of Collective Social Mobility* New York: Croom Helm Ltd.

Patel, N. 1990. A Race against Time. London: Runnymede Trust.

Phillipson, C (1998) *Reconstructing Old Age*, Routledge: London.

Phillipson, C. (1998), *Reconstructing Old Age*. London: Sage.

Phillipson, C. (2006). Ageing and globalization. In J. Vincent, C. Phillipson, & M. Downs (Eds.). *The futures of old age* (pp. 201-207). Thousand Oaks, CA: Sage.

Phillipson, C. 1982. *Capitalism and the Construction of Old Age*. London: Macmillan.

———. 1988. "Challenging Dependency: Towards a New Social Work with Older People." In *Radical Social Work Today*, edited by M. Langan and P. Lee. London: Unwin Hyman.

———. 1998. *Reconstructing Old Age*. London: Sage.

Phillipson, C., and A. Walker, eds. 1986. *Ageing and Social Policy: A Critical Assessment.* Aldershot, U.K.: Gower.

Phillipson, C., and J. L. Powell. 2004. "Risk, Social Welfare and Old Age." In *Old Age and Human Agency*, edited by E. Tulle. Hauppauge, N.Y.: Nova Science Publishers.

Phillipson, C., and S. Biggs. 1998. "Modernity and Identity: Themes and Perspectives in the Study of Older Adults." *Journal of Aging and Identity* 3 (1): 11–23.

Phillipson, C., Bernard, M.; Phillips, J., and Ogg, J. (2000), *The Family and Community Life of Older People*, Rout-ledge: London.

Pillemer, K. and Wolf, R. 1986, *Elder Abuse: Conflict in the Family*, Auburn House: Westport, CT.

Porter, R. 1995 *Medicine in the Enlightenment Amsterdam and Atlanta*.

Porter, R. 1997 *The Greatest Benefit to Mankind: A Medical History of Humanity from Antiquity to the Present London McMillan*.

Powell, J (2005) *Social Theory and Aging*. New York: Rowman and Littlefield.

Powell, J. (2010) *Aging, Theory and Globalization*. Nova Science: NY.

Powell, J. and Cook, I. G. (Eds.) (2010) *Aging in Asia*. Nova Science: NY.

References

Powell, J. (2001), Theorizing Gerontology: The Case of Old Age, Professional Power and Social Policy in the United Kingdom, *Journal of Aging and Identity*, Vol. 6, No. 3, pp. 117-35.

Powell, J. and Biggs, S. (2000), Managing Old Age: The Disciplinary Web of Power and Social Policy in the United Kingdom, *Journal of Aging and Identity*, Vol. 6, No. 3, pp. 117-35.

Powell, J. and Biggs, S. (2000), Managing Old Age: The Disciplinary Web of Power, Surveillance and Normalisation, *Journal of Aging and Identity*, Vol. 5, No. 1, pp. 3-13.

Powell, J. and Cook, I. G. (2000), "A Tiger Behind and Coming Up Fast": Governmentality and the Politics of Population Control in China, *Journal of Aging and Identity*, Vol. 5, No. 2, pp. 79-90.

Powell, J. and Owen, T. 2007, *Reconstructing Postmodernism: Critical Debates*, Nova Science: New York.

Powell, J. L. 1998. *"The "Us" and the "Them": Connecting Political Economy and Foucauldian Insights into Ageing Bodies."* 1–25, *paper presented to the British Sociological Association Annual Conference*, University of Edinburgh.

———. 1999. Review of S. Katz (1996), "Disciplining Old Age: The Formation of Gerontological Knowledge." *Canadian Journal of Sociology* 55 (3): 45–48.

———. 2000. "The Importance of a 'Critical' Sociology of Old Age." *Social Science Paper Publisher* 3 (1): 1–5.

———. 2001a. "The NHS and Community Care Act 1990 in the United Kingdom: A Critical Review between the Years 1981 to 1996." *Sincronia: Journal of Social Sciences and Humanities* 4 (4): 1–10.

———. 2001b. "Social Theory and the Aging Body." *International Journal of Language, Society and Culture* 8 (2): 1–10.

———. 2001c. "Aging and Social Theory: A Sociological Review." *Social Science Paper Publisher* 4 (2): 1–12.

———. 2001d. "Theorizing Gerontology: The Case of Old Age, Professional Power and Social Policy in the United Kingdom." *Journal of Aging & Identity* 6 (3): 117–35.

References

———. 2001e. "Rethinking Structure and Agency: Bio-ethics, Aging and Technologies of the Self." Sincronia: *Journal of Social Sciences and Humanities* 4 (4): 1–10.

———. 2001f. "Women in British Special Hospitals: A Sociological Approach." *Sincronia: Journal of Social Sciences and Humanities* 4 (4): 1–14.

———. 2002. "Archaeology and Genealogy: Developments in Foucauldian Gerontology." *Sincronia: Journal of Social Sciences and Humanities* 5 (1): 1–10.

Powell, J. L., and A. Wahidin. 2003. "Re-configuring Old Bodies: From the Bio-medical Model to a Critical Epistemology." *Journal of Social Sciences and Humanities* 26 (2): 1–10.

———. 2004. "Corporate Crime, Aging and Pensions in Great Britain." *Journal of Societal and Social Policy* 3 (1): 37–55.

Powell, J. L., and C. F. Longino. 2001. "Towards the Postmodernization of Aging: the Body and Social Theory." *Journal of Aging & Identity* 6 (4): 20–34.

———. 2002. "Modernism v. Postmodernism: Rethinking Theoretical Tensions in Social Gerontology." *Journal of Aging Studies* 7 (4): 115–25.

Powell, J. L., and I. Cook. 2000. "'A Tiger Behind and Coming Up Fast': Governmentality and the Politics of Population Control in China." *Journal of Aging & Identity* 5 (2): 79–90.

———. 2001. "Understanding Foucauldian Philosophy: The Case of the Chinese State and the Surveillance of Older People." *International Journal of Language, Society and Culture* 8 (1): 1–9.

Powell, J. L., and J. L. Edwards. 2002. "Policy Narratives of Aging: The Right Way, the Third Way or the Wrong Way?" *Electronic Journal of Sociology* 6 (1): 1–9.

Powell, J. L., and M. M. Edwards. 2003. "Risk and Youth: A Critical Sociological Narrative." *International Journal of Sociology and Social Policy* 23 (12): 81–95.

References

Powell, J. L., and S. Biggs. 2000. "Managing Old Age: The Disciplinary Web of Power, Surveillance and Normalisation." *Journal of Aging and Identity* 5 (1): 3–13.

———. 2003. "Foucauldian Gerontology." *Electronic Journal of Sociology* 7 (3): 1–11.

———. 2004. "Aging, Technologies of Self, and Bio-Medicine: A Foucauldian Excursion." *International Journal of Sociology and Social Policy* 23 (13): 96–115.

Powell, J. L. (2005) *Social Theory and Aging*. Rowman and Littlefield: Lanham.

Powell, J. L. (2009) 'Social Theory, Aging, and Health and Welfare Professionals: A Foucauldian "Toolkit," *Journal of Applied Gerontology,* 28, 6, 669-682.

Powell, J. L. (2011) *Aging, Theory and Globalization*. Nova Science: NY.

Powell, J. L. and Cook, I. (2010) *Aging in Asia.* Nova Science: NY.

Powell, J. L. and Gilbert, T 2010 Power and Social Work in the UK,' *Journal of Social Work*, Vol 8, 1, 321-343.

Power, Surveillance and Normalisation, *Journal of Aging and Identity*, Vol. 5, No. 1, pp. 3-13.

Qualls, S. 1999, Realising Power in Intergenerational Hierachies, in M. Duffy (ed.), *Handbook of Counselling and Psychotherapy with Older Adults*, Wiley: New York.

Rabinow, P., ed. 1984. *The Foucault Reader*. London: Peregrine.

Reddy, S. 1996. "Claims to Expert Knowledge and the Subversion of Democracy: The Triumph of Risk over Uncertainty." *Economy and Society* 25 (2): 222–54.

Riska, E. 2001 *Medical Careers and Feminist Agendas: American*, Scandinavian and Russian Women Physicians London: Sage.

Roberto, K. 1990, Grandparent and Grand-child Relationships, in T. H. Brubaker (ed.), *Family Relationships in Later Life*, Sage: London.

Rose, N. 1993. "Government, Authority, and Expertise in Advanced Liberalism." *Economy and Society* 22 (3): 283–99.

———. 1996. "The Death of the Social? Refiguring the Territory of Government." *Economy and Society* 25 (3): 237–56.

References

103

Rose, N., and P. Miller. 1992. "Political Power beyond the State: Problematics of Government." *British Journal of Sociology* 43 (2): 172–205.

Ryff, C. and Seltzer, M. 1996, *The Parental Experience in Midlife*, Chicago University Press: Chicago, IL.

Sainsbury D. (Ed.). (1994). *Gendering Welfare States.* Thousand Oaks, CA: Sage.

Sainsbury, D. (1996). *Gender equality and welfare states.* Cambridge: Cambridge University Press.

Saraga, E., ed. 1998. *Embodying the Social: Constructions of Difference.* London: Routledge.

Satyamurti, C. 1974. "Women's Occupation and Social Change: The Case of Social Work." *Paper presented to 1974 British Sociological Association's Annual Conference.*

Scarfe, G. 1993. *Scarface.* London: Sinclaire-Stevenson.

Scharf, T. and Wenger, G. 1995, *International Perspectives on Community Care for Older People*, Avebury: Al-dershot, UK.

Scheiwe, K. (1994). German pension insurance, gendered times and stratification. In D. Sainsbury (Ed.). *Gendering Welfare States* (pp. 132-149). Thousand Oaks, CA: Sage.

Schrag, P. 1980. *Mind Control.* New York: Marion Bowyars.

Schreck, H. 2000, *Community and Caring*, UPA: New York.

Seidman, S. 1994. *Contested Knowledge: Social Theory in the Postmodern Era.* Oxford: Blackwell.

Shalev, M. (2007). Book review of G. J. Kasza *One world of welfare: Japan in comparative perspective.* In *American Journal of Sociology, 112,* 905-907.

Shilling, C. 1993. *The Body & Social Theory.* London: Sage.

Shumway, D. 1989. *Michel Foucault.* Charlottesville: University Press of Virginia.

Silverstein, M. and Bengtson, V. L. 1997, Intergenerational Solidarity and the Structure of Adult Child-Parent Relationships in American Families, *American Journal of Sociology*, Vol. 103, No. 2, pp. 429-60.

References

Sim, J., et al. eds. 1987. *Law, Order and the Authoritarian State*. Milton Keynes, U.K.: Oxford University Press.

Sinclair, S. 1997 *Making Doctors: An Institutional Apprenticeship* London: Berg.

Siraisis, N. 1990 *Medieval and Early Renaissance Medicine: An Introduction to Knowledge and Practice Chicago*: Chicago University Press.

Smart, B. 1985. *Michel Foucault*. London: Routledge.

————. 1993. *Postmodernity*. London: Routledge.

Sontag, S. 1978. "The Double Standard of Ageing." In *An Ageing Population*, edited by V. Carver and P. Liddiard. Milton Keynes, U.K.: Oxford University Press.

————. 1991. *Illness as Metaphor and AIDS and Its Metaphors*. London: Penguin.

Steger, M. B. (1997). The future of globalization. In A. D. King (Ed.). *Culture, globalization and the World-System* (pp. 116-129), Minneapolis, MN: University of Minnesota Press.

Steger, M. B. (1997). The future of globalization. In A. D. King (Ed.). *Culture, globalization and the World-System* (pp. 116-129), Minneapolis, MN: University of Minnesota Press.

Steuerman, E. 1992. "Habermas vs. Lyotard: Modernity vs. Postmodernity?" In *Judging Lyotard*, edited by A. Benjamin. London: Routledge.

Stott, M. 1981. *Ageing for Beginners*. Oxford: Blackwell.

Tekula, Rebecca (2010). Social Enterprise: Innovation or Mission Distraction? *Working Chapter, Helene and Grant Wilson Center for Social Entrepreneurship*, Pace University.

Tekula, Rebecca (2010). Social Enterprise: Innovation or Mission Distraction? *Working Chapter, Helene and Grant Wilson Center for Social Entrepreneurship*, Pace University.

Tenkin, O. 1973 *Galenism: Rise and Decline of a Medical Philosophy* Ithaca: NY.

Thompson, E. P. 1967. "Time, Work—Discipline and Industrial Capitalism." *Past and Present* 38:56–97.

References 105

Thompson, K. 1992. "Social Pluralism and Postmodernity." In *Modernity and Its Futures*, edited by S. Hall, D. Held, and T. McGrew. Cambridge: Polity.

Thompson, P. 1999, The Role of Grandparents When Parents Part or Die: Some Reflections on the Mythical Decline of the Extended Family, *Ageing and Society*, Vol. 19, No. 4, pp. 471-503.

Thomson, E. and Minkler, M. 2001, American Grandparents Providing Extensive Childcare to Their Grand-children: Prevalence and Profile, *The Gerontologist*, Vol. 41, No. 2, pp. 201-09.

Timiras, P., ed. 1997. *Physiological Basis of Aging and Geriatrics*. 2nd ed. Paris: Masson.

Tinker, A. 1997. *Older People in Modern Society*. London: Longman.

Townsend, P. (2007). Using human rights to defeat ageism: Dealing with policy-induced 'structured dependency.' In M. Bernard & T. Scharf (Eds.), *Critical perspectives on ageing societies* (pp. 27-44). Bristol, UK: Polity Press.

Townsend, P. (2007). Using human rights to defeat ageism: Dealing with policy-induced 'structured dependency.' In M. Bernard & T. Scharf (Eds.), *Critical perspectives on ageing societies* (pp. 27-44). Bristol, UK: Polity Press.

Townsend, P. 1981. "The Structured Dependency of the Elderly: A Creation of Social Policy in the Twentieth Century." *Ageing and Society* 1 (1): 5–28.

Townsend, P., and D. Wedderburn. 1965. *The Aged in the Welfare State*. London: Bell.

Toyota, M. (2006), *Ageing and transnational householding: Japanese retirees in Southeast Asia, International Development Planning Review*, 28, 4: 515-531.

Tulle-Winton, E. 1999. "Growing Old and Resistance: Towards a New Cultural Economy of Old Age?" *Ageing and Society* 19:281–99.

Tulloch, J., and D. Lupton. 2003. *Risk and Everyday Life*. London: Sage.

Turner, B. S. 1989. "Ageing, Status Politics and Sociological Theory." *British Journal of Sociology* 40:588–606.

References

Turner, B. S. 1995 *Medical Power and Social Knowledge* London: Sage Publications.

———. 1995. "Ageing and Identity." In *Images of Ageing*, edited by M. Featherstone and A. Wernick. London: Routledge.

Twigg, J. 2000. "Social Policy and the Body." In *Rethinking Social Policy*, edited by G. Lewis, S. Gewirtz, and J. Clarke. London: Sage.

UKG, UK Government 1981, *Growing Older*, HMSO: London.

UKG, UK Government 1989, *Community Care: An Agenda for Action*, HMSO: London.

UKG, UK Government 1990, *NHS and Community Care Act*, HMSO: London.

UKG, UK Government 1993, *No Longer Afraid: The Safeguard of Older People in Domestic Settings*, HMSO: London.

UKG, UK Government 2000a, *Winning the Generation Game*, www.cabinet-office.gov.uk.

UKG, UK Government 2000b, *Supporting Families*, HMSO: London.

United Nations Department of Economic and Social Affair (2002) *Population Division. World Population Ageing 1950–2050.* New York: United Nations.

Veyne, P. 1980. *Foucault revolutionne l'histoire*. Paris: Éditions Seuil.

Victor, C. 1987. *Old Age in Modern Society*. London: Croom Helm.

Vincent, J. 1996. *Inequality and Old Age*. London: University College London Press.

Vincent, J. 1999. *Politics, Power and Old Age*. Buckingham: Open University Press.

Virilio, P. 1983. *Pure War*. New York: Semiotext.

Visker, R. 1995. *Michel Foucault*. Verso: London.

Wade, R. H. (2007). The causes of increasing world poverty and inequality; or, what the Matthew Effect prevails. In V. Navarro (Ed.), *Neoliberalism, globalization and inequalities: Consequences for health and quality of life* (pp. 119-141). Amityville, NY: Baywood.

Wahidin, A., and J. L. Powell. 2001. "The Loss of Aging Identity: Social Theory, Old Age and the Power of Special Hospitals." *Journal of Aging & Identity* 6 (1): 31–49.

References

107

———. 2003. "Reconfiguring Old Bodies: From the Biomedical Model to a Critical Epistemology." *Journal of Social Sciences and Humanities* 26 (2): 1–10.

Waldrop, D., Weber, J., Herald, S., Pruett, J., Cooper, K., and Jouzapavicius, K. (1999), Wisdom and Life Experience: How Grandfathers Mentor Their Grandchildren, *Journal of Aging and Identity*, Vol. 4, No. 1, pp. 33-46.

Walker, A. 2002, A Strategy for Active Ageing, *International Social Security Review*, Vol. 55, No. 1, pp. 121-39.

Walker, A. and Naeghele, G. (2000) *The Politics of Ageing in Europe*. OUP: Milton Keynes.

Walker, A. 1981. "Towards a Political Economy of Old Age." *Ageing and Society* 1:73–94.

———. 1985. *The Care Gap: How Can Local Authorities Meet the Needs of the Elderly?* London: Local Government Information Unit.

———. 1987. "The Social Construction of Dependency in Old Age." In *The State or the Market?* edited by M. Loney, 41–57. London: Sage.

———. 1990. "Poverty and Inequality in Old Age." In *Ageing and Society*, edited by J. Bond and P. Coleman. London: Sage.

Walker, A. and Aspalter, C. 2008, *Securing the Future for Old Age in Europe*, Casa Verde: Hong Kong.

Walker, A., and G. Naeghele. 1999. *The Politics of Old Age in Europe*. Milton Keynes, U.K.: Oxford University Press.

Warnes, A., ed. 1996. *Human Ageing and Later Life*. London: Edward Arnold.

Watts, J. (2006), 'Online Survey Axed After Most Reject Chinese Identity, *Guardian*, 19th September.

Wenger, C. 1984, *Support Networks for Older People*, CSPRD: Bangor, UK.

Wilkinson, I. 2001. "Social Theories of Risk Perception: At Once Indispensable and Insufficient." *Current Sociology* 49 (1): 1–22.

Williams, F. 1994. *Social Policy: A Critical Introduction*, 2nd ed. Oxford: Blackwell.

References

World Bank (1994), *Averting the Old-Age Crisis*, Oxford University Press: Oxford, UK.

Wynne, B. 1987. *Risk Management and Hazardous Waste*. Berlin: Springer.

Yapa, L. (2002). Globalization and poverty: From a poststructural perspective. In B. I. Logan (Ed.). *Globalization, the third world state and poverty-alleviation in the twenty-first century* (pp. 15-29). Aldershot, UK: Ashgate.

Zheng, L. (2004), China Faces Elderly Dilemma, *China Daily*, August 21.

Authors' Contact Information

Jason L. Powell

Associate Dean of Health and Social Care,
Staffordshire University, UK
Email: jasonpwll3@gmail.com

Sheying Chen

Professor
Pace University, New York, NY, US
Email: sheyingchen@yahoo.com

INDEX

#

20th century, 71
21st century, 68, 69, 74, 78

A

adolescents, 19
adults, 14, 20, 32, 52, 54, 57, 59, 60, 63
aging, v, vii, ix, 1, 2, 3, 4, 5, 6, 7, 8, 9, 12,
13, 14, 15, 16, 17, 19, 20, 21, 23, 24, 25,
29, 30, 31, 32, 33, 34, 37, 38, 39, 40, 41,
42, 43, 44, 45, 46, 47, 48, 49, 50, 51, 52,
53, 55, 56, 57, 58, 59, 63, 64, 65, 77, 80,
81, 82, 83, 84, 85,87, 90, 92, 94, 95, 96,
97, 98, 99, 100, 101, 102, 105, 106, 107
aging identity, ix, 21, 32, 39, 48, 49, 64, 106
aging population, 5, 13, 52, 96
aging process, 2
anthropology, 95
Asia, 65, 84, 92, 99, 102
attitudes, 2, 3, 9, 10, 15

B

biological science, 1
biomedical model, 1, 9, 17, 22, 33, 107
biotechnology, 43, 44, 45, 46
black women, 15, 16
Britain, 54, 55, 77, 79, 82, 86

C

China, 65, 82, 84, 85, 86, 87, 90, 91, 92, 96,
98, 100, 101, 108
chronic illness, 40
climate change, ix
community, 7, 10, 18, 19, 36, 52, 54, 56, 59,
64
cultural values, 16
culture, 1, 15, 17, 18, 19, 21, 24, 25, 29, 30,
31, 34, 35, 36, 43, 45, 46, 47, 84

D

democratization, 29
demographic change, 5, 9, 57

112 *Index*

denial, 21, 37, 42
developed countries, 66
developing countries, 75
digital divide, 70, 74

E

early retirement, 32
East Asia, 95
Eastern Europe, 65
economic change, 70
economic development, 73, 77
economic disadvantage, 11
economic downturn, 78
economic growth, 28
economic integration, 75
economic policy, 4
economic power, 78
economic problem, 10
economic reform, 73
economic relations, 69
economics, 14, 69
elders, 18, 45, 53, 55, 58
embodiment, vii, ix, 1, 23, 24, 25, 39, 40, 42, 83, 96
employability, 71
employment, 6, 15, 55, 67, 71, 73
employment opportunities, 67
ethnic groups, 17, 38, 61
ethnicity, 13, 16, 33, 66
Europe, 17, 51, 53, 69, 80, 94, 96, 107
everyday life, 3, 23, 25, 50

F

families, 13, 18, 19, 50, 52, 53, 54, 55, 56, 57, 58, 60, 62, 63
family life, 32, 50, 51, 54, 56, 63
family members, 20, 64, 74
family system, 19, 60
family therapy, 59

feminism, 17, 24, 30
feminist gerontology, 4, 20, 23, 39, 41
Foucault, Michel, iii, iv
functionalism, 8, 9, 16, 17, 20, 23, 39
functionalist gerontology, 4

G

Germany, 54, 56, 61, 66
gerontologists, ix, 5, 31, 33, 42, 55
gerontology, 1, 2, 3, 4, 5, 8, 11, 13, 16, 20, 21, 23, 24, 28, 29, 30, 31, 32, 33, 39, 40, 41, 42, 44, 47, 48, 49
globalization, 47, 54, 68, 69, 70, 71, 74, 76, 77, 79, 80, 86, 92, 95, 96, 98, 99, 104, 106
Great Britain, 5, 18, 101

H

health, 4, 17, 18, 19, 31, 35, 66, 73, 86, 98, 106
health care, 17, 73
human agency, 11, 20
human behavior, 2
human body, 33, 43, 48
human rights, 105
human sciences, 24
humanism, 43

I

identity, ix, 1, 2, 4, 14, 16, 20, 21, 24, 30, 31, 32, 35, 39, 42, 43, 44, 46, 48, 49, 50, 60, 63, 64, 73, 74, 86, 87, 90, 91, 96, 99, 100, 101, 102, 106, 107
individual perception, 36
individualism, 30, 52, 71, 74
individuals, ix, 2, 3, 6, 10, 11, 12, 16, 17, 21, 26, 29, 30, 49, 51, 65, 71

Index

interpersonal relationships, 50
intervention, 11, 12, 75
intimacy, 59

J

Japan, 61, 66, 103

K

Keynes, 79, 81, 82, 83, 87, 88, 93, 97, 104, 107

L

labor market, 16, 66, 67, 71, 75, 78
later life, 31, 32, 34, 42, 45, 63, 64
Latin America, 65
life course, 2, 75
life satisfaction, 8
loneliness, 32

M

marginalization, 10, 15, 16, 21
medical, 2, 5, 9, 18, 25, 34, 42, 43, 44, 73, 101
medicine, 1, 43, 83, 96
mental model, 76
mentor, 57, 58
mentoring, 56
metaphor, 36
models, 4, 9, 19, 20, 32, 49, 74
models of aging, 4, 20
Modern Age, 90
modern society, 8, 12, 26
modernity, 4, 11, 12, 20, 24, 25, 26, 28, 30, 43, 48

N

neoliberalism, 11, 12, 13, 51, 62
Netherlands, 91
NGOs, 68, 72, 74, 77
North America, 30, 54
nursing home, 20, 31

O

old age, vii, 1, 4, 5, 7, 8, 9, 10, 11, 14, 16, 19, 23, 31, 37, 39, 40, 41, 45, 51, 59, 62, 66, 79, 82, 85, 86, 87, 93, 94, 98, 99, 100, 102, 105, 106, 107
oppression, 15, 29, 47

P

physical and mental, 1
physical characteristics, 17
policy, ix, 4, 5, 12, 44, 50, 51, 52, 53, 54, 55, 56, 57, 58, 59, 60, 62, 63, 66, 68, 69, 76, 84, 92, 93, 96, 105
policy initiative, 52, 55
population, 18, 55, 62, 65, 66, 72, 76, 97
population control, 65
population group, 18
positive aging, 7, 58
positivism, 30
postmodernism, 21, 25, 30, 45, 47, 48, 49
poverty, 4, 10, 12, 16, 48, 65, 75, 77, 80, 106, 108
power, ii, iii, iv
power relations, 2, 8, 15, 26, 35, 43, 47
psychological well-being, 6
public welfare, 75, 76

Q

quality of life, 66, 86, 98, 106

Index

R

race, 4, 5, 8, 13, 16, 17, 20, 21, 42, 62, 82, 85, 99
resources, 8, 9, 10, 11, 12, 14, 20, 69, 71, 75, 84

S

scarce resources, 44, 73
services, vi, 9, 10, 12, 16, 18, 44, 53, 71, 75, 77, 85
sexuality, 4, 16, 19, 20, 34, 89
social construction, vii, 1, 2, 12, 21, 23, 91, 107
social constructs, 2, 21
social context, 3, 21
social exclusion, 62, 66
social expenditure, 9, 70
social fabric, 53
social gerontology, 1, 3, 4, 16, 28, 29, 31, 33, 40, 42, 49, 79, 81, 101
social group, 16, 57
social identity, 42
social inequalities, 83
social interaction, 2
social justice, 17, 28, 68, 70, 77
social network, 19, 61
social order, 24, 30
social organization, 20
social phenomena, 5
social policy, 4, 11, 50, 54, 62, 63, 66, 69, 86, 88, 95, 96
social problems, 10, 20, 23
social relations, 6, 21, 23, 51, 68
social relationships, 6, 21
social roles, 23
social rules, 27
social safety nets, 73
Social Security, 16, 54, 86, 91, 107

social services, 16, 18, 72
social structure, 3, 10, 14
social theory, 4, 8, 21, 26, 29, 42, 46, 47, 48
social welfare, 13, 17, 66, 69, 70, 75, 77
society, ix, 2, 3, 4, 6, 7, 8, 9, 10, 11, 12, 14, 15, 16, 17, 19, 20, 22, 24, 26, 28, 29, 32, 33, 35, 38, 42, 43, 46, 47, 54, 56, 57, 71, 74, 84
socio-economic issues, ix
sociology of aging, 2, 3, 4
Sweden, 66
Switzerland, 95

T

theory-method dualism, 1
transnational corporations, 71

U

United Kingdom, 9, 13, 50, 53, 54, 56, 59, 60, 61, 62, 100
United Nations, 106
United States, 5, 6, 9, 16, 17, 53, 56, 60, 61, 66, 97

V

vulnerability, 15, 37

W

welfare, 5, 9, 10, 11, 12, 13, 52, 53, 66, 68, 70, 75, 76, 77, 78, 80, 86, 87, 88, 97, 103
welfare state, 5, 68, 77, 78, 87, 88, 97, 103
Western culture, 1, 17, 19, 31, 35
workers, 19, 56, 71, 72
working population, 56

Related Nova Publications

Life Course and Society

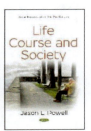

Author: Jason L. Powell

Series: Social Perspectives in the 21st Century

Book Description: This book explores the concept of key concepts, theories and practices related to life course issues associated with social work, power and trust in contemporary society.

Softcover ISBN: 978-1-53613-848-1
Retail Price: $82

The Power of Global Aging

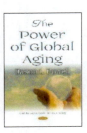

Author: Jason L. Powell

Series: Social Perspectives in the 21st Century

Book Description: This book is a demographical overview of the key issues associated with globalisation and global aging in the 21st century. The book explores how populational aging has increased the implications for socio-economic issues for individuals and populations.

Softcover ISBN: 978-1-53613-846-7
Retail Price: $82

To see a complete list of Nova publications, please visit our website at www.novapublishers.com